D1765993

hexagons made easy

machine techniques for exceptional quilts

Jen Eskridge

Martingale®
Create with Confidence

Hexagons Made Easy: Machine Techniques
for Exceptional Quilts
© 2013 by Jen Eskridge

Martingale®
19021 120th Ave. NE, Ste. 102
Bothell, WA 98011-9511 USA
ShopMartingale.com

No part of this product may be reproduced in any form,
unless otherwise stated, in which case reproduction
is limited to the use of the purchaser. The written
instructions, photographs, designs, projects, and
patterns are intended for the personal, noncommercial
use of the retail purchaser and are under federal
copyright laws; they are not to be reproduced by any
electronic, mechanical, or other means, including
informational storage or retrieval systems, for commercial
use. Permission is granted to photocopy patterns for the
personal use of the retail purchaser. Attention teachers:
Martingale encourages you to use this book for teaching,
subject to the restrictions stated above.

The information in this book is presented in good
faith, but no warranty is given nor results guaranteed.
Since Martingale has no control over choice of materials
or procedures, the company assumes no responsibility
for the use of this information.

Printed in China
18 17 16 15 14 13   8 7 6 5 4 3 2 1

Library of Congress Cataloging-in-Publication Data
is available upon request.

ISBN: 978-1-60468-275-5

Mission Statement

Dedicated to providing quality products
and service to inspire creativity.

Credits

President & CEO: Tom Wierzbicki
Editor in Chief: Mary V. Green
Design Director: Paula Schlosser
Managing Editor: Karen Costello Soltys
Acquisitions Editor: Karen M. Burns
Technical Editor: Nancy Mahoney
Copy Editor: Tiffany Mottet
Production Manager: Regina Girard
Illustrator: Rose Sheifer
Cover & Text Designer: Regina Girard
Photographer: Brent Kane

contents

introduction

Welcome to a whole new way of creating hexagons for a variety of quilts and other sewing projects! Fundamentally, my technique is to accurately stitch a facing to all sides of a geometric shape and then turn the piece right side out, yielding a finished shape with edges neatly folded under and smooth on all sides. Although the projects in this book are all hexagon-based, my technique can be applied to any geometric shape.

While inspired by English paper piecing, my facing technique goes above and beyond hand-sewing methods. Hexagons can be appliquéd to a quilt block or quilt top, or they can be joined together for a reversible quilt. You can create designs ranging from pillows and table runners to queen-size quilts, any of which can be assembled in a weekend. This technique also allows you to work with various sizes of hexagons as well as different types of fabrics beyond quilting cottons.

Why *Faced* Hexagons?

Old is the *new* new! Like fashion, quilting seems to be cyclical, and currently we're enjoying a resurgence of interest in hexagons. The shape is showing up in many modern and traditional designs, and can be created a variety of different ways.

Traditionally, hexagons are pieced together by hand sewing or carefully machine sewing Y-seams, which are created when three seam lines meet to form a point or Y. This type of seam is recommended for a patient, more-advanced sewist. English paper piecing is another way to make hexagons, but this very popular method relies heavily on hand sewing to prepare and join the shapes. In both methods, the finished quilt top also needs to be quilted. Neither method offers quick finishing techniques.

Although both Y-seams and English paper piecing produce beautiful results, each has its drawbacks, from skill level to time constraints. I wanted a way to yield a similar look with an easier, faster method—namely, a facing.

By facing the hexagons, you'll have the freedom to expand on the already-fabulous hexagon designs. You'll be able to make a hexagon (or other shape) as large as you can dream. This would be quite difficult with English paper-piecing methods. Individual hexagons in this book range from 2" to 24" diagonally.

Additionally, with my methods, you can make a hexagon or another shape from *any* fabric type, including lightweight silk, which would normally fray from overhandling. The machine-stitched facing makes quick work of turning under the raw edges, so fraying is a not an issue. You can also use stiff burlap or decorator-weight fabrics, which would definitely not be suitable for hand sewing or Y-seam construction.

Lastly, you'll be able to make projects quickly. Once the hexagons are faced, you can machine appliqué them to a background or join them together for a reversible project that needs no quilting or binding.

How to Use This Book

This book is divided into five sections: techniques, blocks, block-based quilt ideas, whole-cloth quilts and coverlets, and home-decor projects.

In "The Techniques" (page 6), you'll find basic instructions for making faced hexagons. "The Blocks" (page 21) offers you 18 block designs that you can mix and match. In "Block-Based Quilt Ideas" (page 37), you'll find ideas for using the blocks to make interesting multi-block or sampler-style quilts. "Whole-Cloth Quilts and Coverlets" (page 41) touches on two styles of quilts using faced hexagons—whole-cloth quilts with appliquéd hexagons, and coverlets made by joining reversible hexagons. Both methods are quick and will allow

you to expand your quiltmaking skills. "Home-Decor Projects" (page 63) shows you ways to incorporate hexagons into pillows, table runners, and party decorations.

You can use my facing method for any geometric shape. Go forth and make giant triangles, huge octagons, and tons of reversible polygons! The only boundary is your imagination.

This book also focuses on unique, modern-looking projects. After you are comfortable with the process, feel free to adapt the facing method to your other hexagon-based quilt patterns, such as a traditional Grandmother's Flower Garden quilt.

Grandmother's Flower Garden quilt from the 1930s.

I'm confident, once you get the hang of making a faced geometric shape, the creative ideas will flow. Use this book as a springboard to the endless possibilities of faced shapes.

Before diving into the technique process, I'll start by reviewing the basic supplies and sewing terms. Then we'll take a look at the methods, step by step. Once the methods are broken down, you'll see the process is quite easy.

Basic Supplies

As with any type of quiltmaking or craft projects, making faced hexagons involves a few basic tools and supplies. Here's what you'll need:

- Iron
- Non-permanent pen or marker (I use a FriXion Pen)*
- Scissors
- Sewing machine
- Template material, such as cardstock, plastic, or cardboard
- Thread
- Turning tool to make crisp points; a wooden chopstick works well
- Rotary cutting supplies (optional)
- Inklingo hexagon printing software (optional)
- AccuQuilt Go! Hexagon Dies (optional)

Ideally you'll want to use something non-permanent, such as chalk or a water-soluble marker. However, in the case of heavy burlap or home decorator fabric, a felt-tip marker works well.

Basic Sewing Terms

Let's review basic terms before diving straight into the how-to of my methods.

Bias and Grain Line

These terms refer to the direction of the fabric's woven threads. *On grain* means the edge of a piece is cut parallel to the fabric weave, resulting in 90° cuts. *True bias* is a cut made at a 45° angle, relative to the fabric weave. When a piece or shape has bias edges, the fabric has a tendency to stretch or skew during the sewing steps. It's important to know that hexagons have four bias edges. These edges are

60° angles, not true bias. They're not as stretchy as true bias edges, but they can stretch out of shape if not handled carefully. When sewing these bias edges, sew slowly and don't pull the shapes as your machine feeds the fabric under the needle.

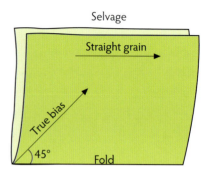

Facings

Facing is an apparel-construction term referring to the fabric sewn to a garment element to conceal the raw fabric edges and give the element its structure. Facings are commonly used in collars, cuffs, lapels, necklines, and shaped hems.

In quilting and home decor, we sew a piece of facing fabric to a predetermined shape for the purpose of finishing or turning under the raw edges of the shape to hide the seam allowances.

Clipping and Trimming

Clipping and trimming is generally done when applying a facing to reduce bulk in the seam allowances and create crisp corners. When clipping, you will remove the excess fabric in the seam allowances near a corner.

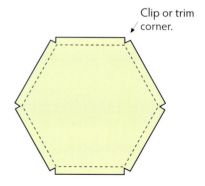

● facing fabric choices

With any faced piece, there are two main considerations for appropriate facing fabric: fabric weight and end use.

Fabric weight varies by style of fabric, from lightweight silk and cotton, to heavyweight canvas and burlap. You may want to choose a different type of fabric weight depending on whether the facing will be seen (reversible hexagons), or if it will be hidden (appliquéd hexagons). When using lightweight cottons and silks, the weight of the facing fabric should be similar to that of the focus fabric (the fabric on the front that you'll see).

When using decorator-weight fabrics, choose a sturdier facing fabric. You can create a sturdier fabric by applying fusible or sew-in interfacing to a lightweight facing fabric. For burlap, choose a fabric that is a bit heavier, but looks the same on the front and back (such as a dyed solid or yarn-dyed woven fabric), since the facing will be slightly visible though the loose weave of the burlap focus fabric.

End uses vary quite a lot and will require specific facing needs.

● **Reversible projects:** The facing should be comparable in weight and quality to the fabric used on the "front" of the project, since, technically, both sides are the front. (See "Lap Coverlet" on page 59.)

● **Appliqué:** You'll make your best effort to conceal the facing fabric when you appliqué the hexagon to the quilt, but to ensure it blends into the finished project, use a facing fabric with a similar color. Lightweight facings are ideal as they won't add extra bulk to the quilt top. (See "Hexagon Circle" on page 42.)

● **Washability and shrinkage:** Match the fiber content when possible so the project can be easily washed and cared for without uneven or unexpected shrinking.

● **Function:** Consider using a performance fabric for the facing, such as a heavy flannel in a coverlet for warmth or Insul-Fleece in a table runner for heat resistance. According to the project's function, you can also use flannel, Insul-Fleece, or other interfacings *in addition to* facing.

While the facing technique will work for any geometric shape, you may want to avoid shapes with acute or sharp angles. Very pointy shapes require a shorter stitch length when applying the facing and additional care in removing fabric bulk from the seam allowances.

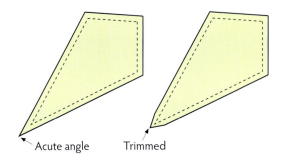

Acute angle   Trimmed

Use either rotary cutting tools or scissors to remove the excess fabric beyond the stitching line by trimming the seam allowances to ¼" or ½" wide depending on the project end use and size. Trimming the focus-fabric seam allowance and the facing seam allowance to different widths, within ⅛" of each other, will allow the seam allowances to lay staggered inside the shape and will not produce a ridge or lump around the perimeter. This staggering is called *grading* the seam allowances.

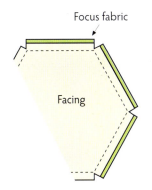

Focus fabric

Facing

Favoring

Favoring is an apparel-construction term where the focus fabric is rolled ever-so-slightly (1⁄16" or less) toward the facing side during the pressing step. This gentle pull and press ensures that the facing is not seen from the right side of the project piece. The most effective way to press and favor the shape is to press with the facing side of the shape on top.

Appliqué

Appliqué means *applying* a fabric or shape to a background fabric. For appliqué projects, I recommend machine appliqué methods. There are at least four layers of fabric along the outer edge of each faced shape, not including any interfacing, fleece, or performance fabric. This bulk is quite difficult to sew through by hand.

A straight stitch around the edge of the shape will give a neat, tidy finish to the appliquéd shape.

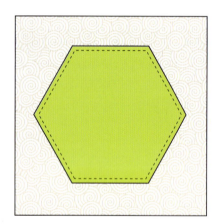

Straight-stitch appliqué

If your sewing machine has decorative stitch capabilities, a narrow blind-hem stitch and monofilament will give an invisible look to the appliqué.

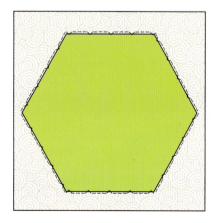

Blind hem stitch

Any decorative machine stitch, such as a blanket stitch, may also be used around the edges of the finished shapes to apply the shapes to the background. This will give a more traditional feel to the design.

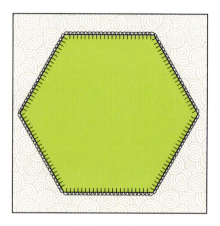

Blanket stitch

Facing Construction Methods

Hexagon sizes are generally referred to in one of two ways: either by the length of one side of a hexagon, or the measurement (or diameter) between two straight sides. The quilt industry relies heavily on the length method, while computer software used to generate hexagons uses the diameter method. Throughout this book, I consistently use a *diagonal* diameter, or the measurement between two opposite points, to describe hexagon sizes. However, in many projects, the exact dimension isn't critical as long as the size is consistent. I find it easier to plan background sizes when using the diagonal point-to-point measurement, because it shows about how much space the hexagon will fill.

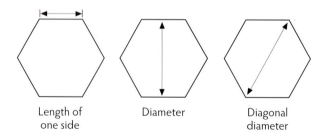

Length of one side   Diameter   Diagonal diameter

Making a Hexagon Template

Determine what size hexagon you need and trace it onto template material. Templates can be made from cardstock, template paper or plastic, poster board, or even recycled cereal boxes. The size of the template represents the exact size of the shape you're making *without* seam allowances. After tracing the shapes onto your fabric, you'll sew exactly on the marked line. Take the time to make an accurate template, as it is the base for the entire project.

Other quick options for making hexagons include an AccuQuilt fabric-cutting system. AccuQuilt offers three different sizes (2", 3", and 5") of hexagon dies, which make incredibly quick work of the cutting and trimming processes. When using a die, the ¼"-wide seam allowance is included in the shape.

Another option is offered through Inklingo. This company produces software that prints the shape, including the cutting and stitching lines, directly onto the wrong side of your fabric. In addition to the software, you'll need an ordinary inkjet printer. This process makes marking hexagons a breeze.

Drafting Large Hexagons

If you want to use a large hexagon (I often use 15"-diameter hexagons), you'll need a way to draft a larger pattern. You can use Photoshop or my easy method for drawing a hexagon from an asterisk.

Using Photoshop. If you have a Photoshop program on your computer, you can use it to draft shapes. This process may take some practice!

1. Open a new file in Photoshop. The width and height in inches will be determined by what size hexagon you want to create. For example, if you want a 15"-diameter hexagon, set the width at 16" and the height at 16". The resolution should be 100 pixels per inch. Click on "OK."
2. On the left toolbar, click on the Polygon tool. Then, in the top toolbar, change the number of sides to six.
3. Drag the cursor over the workspace to create a large shape in the space. Note: If the shape's edges extend beyond the edges of the workspace, click the Move tool in the left toolbar to drag the shape to the center of the workspace.
4. Click on "Layer," then "Rasterize," and then "Shape." This will fill your shape with the foreground color and make it usable for printing and easy manipulation.

5. Save the file as a JPEG. The background will be on one layer and the hexagon will be on a second layer. If given the option to "Flatten image?" click on "OK." This will keep the file small, making it easier to work with.

⬡ printing

I recommend coloring the hexagon outline a very pale gray and the background white to save ink when printing. Files and shapes larger than the standard paper size will print on multiple sheets and need to be taped together for use.

Drafting manually. If the Photoshop option isn't available to you, use the asterisk pattern on page 10 to manually draft a larger hexagon. Each arm of the asterisk represents a point on a hexagon.

1. Copy or trace the asterisk pattern and tape the copied page in the center of a large poster board or sheet of template paper.

Asterisk shape

2. Using a straight edge, such as a yard stick or large acrylic ruler, extend each arm of the asterisk.
3. Measure your desired length on each arm and make a mark. Remember, each arm is half the size of the finished hexagon. For example, to make a 20"-diameter hexagon, each arm needs to be 10" long.

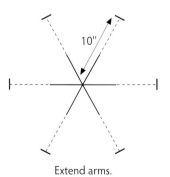

Extend arms.

4. Use the straight edge to connect the marked dots, completing a perfect large hexagon. Cut out the shape to use as your template.

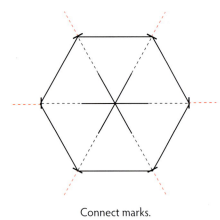

Connect marks.

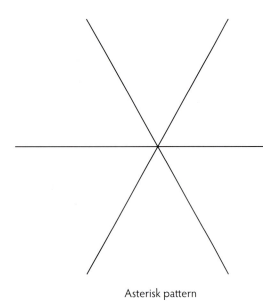

Asterisk pattern

Preparing the Facing Hexagons

1. Using your hexagon template and a non-permanent marker, trace the shape onto the *wrong* side of the facing fabric.

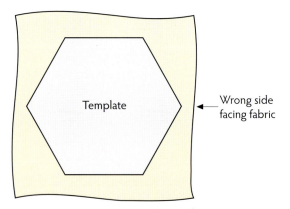

Template

← Wrong side facing fabric

⬡ multiple hexagons

When you need more than one hexagon from the same piece of fabric, trace the number of shapes needed onto the wrong side of the fabric, leaving ¾" between each shape to allow for seam allowances. *Do not* cut the shapes apart; simply pin the group of hexagons to the right side of the focus fabric. You'll cut the shapes apart *after* sewing on the line as described in "Stitching the Hexagons" (page 11).

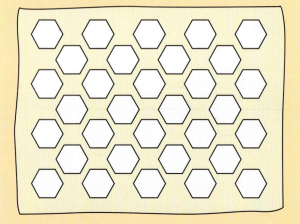

Multiple hexagons traced onto facing fabric

2. Roughly cut out the shape, leaving a margin of about ½" all around the marked line. The actual seam allowance will be trimmed after the piece is sewn. *Don't cut on the marked line* or the hexagon will be ½" smaller after it's stitched.

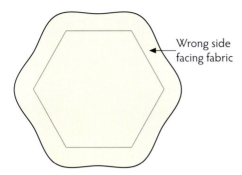

Wrong side facing fabric

3. Place the facing fabric on the focus fabric, right sides together, and pin in place. The marked hexagon should be facing up.

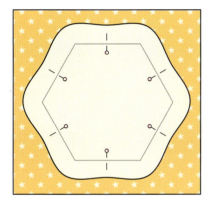

Stitching the Hexagons

Whether the facing will be seen in a reversible design or hidden, as in an appliquéd design, will determine how the hexagons are stitched. Be sure to use a small to medium stitch length to ensure the corners will not fray.

Reversible Hexagons

With reversible hexagons, both sides of the hexagon will show in the finished project.

1. Sewing on the marked line, stitch around the shape as shown. Leave an opening in the center of one side, making sure to stitch each corner. Backstitch along each side of the opening.

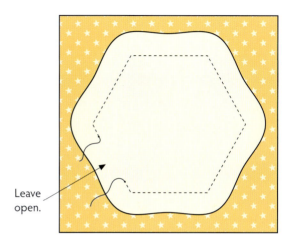

Leave open.

2. Clip each corner to remove excess fabric in the seam allowances. Trim and grade the seam allowances as described in "Clipping and Trimming" (page 6).

3. Turn the hexagon right side out. Use a turning tool to push out the points to make a nice crisp shape. Tuck in the seam allowances along the open edge and press the facing slightly. Do not favor either side of the hexagon, as you would with a facing (see "Favoring" on page 8). Since both sides are the "right side," no favoring is required.

4. Pin the opening closed. All projects provide a method for machine sewing the opening closed. If none of these methods fit your design, consider hand sewing the opening using a blind stitch.

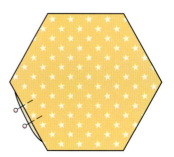

Appliquéd Hexagons

For appliquéd hexagons, the facing fabric is hidden. Use a small to medium stitch length to ensure the corners will not fray.

1. Starting and stopping with a backstitch, sew on the marked line around the entire shape.
2. Clip each corner to remove excess fabric in the seam allowances. Trim and grade the seam allowances as described in "Clipping and Trimming" (page 6).
3. Gently pull the facing away from the focus fabric and make a small snip in the facing fabric about 1" from the stitching line. Cut away the facing fabric, cutting parallel to the stitching line and leaving roughly 1" of facing fabric around the entire shape. (When removing the facing from a large shape, cut carefully so you'll be able to reuse the facing fabric for a smaller shape.)

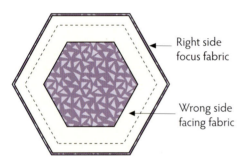

Right side focus fabric

Wrong side facing fabric

4. Turn the shape right side out. Use a turning tool to push out the points to make a nice crisp shape. Press and favor the facing (see "Favoring" on page 8).

Facing Large Hexagons

Very large hexagons require quite a bit of facing fabric, especially if you're making enough for a bed-sized quilt. Here's a way to get the same results while using less fabric.

1. Trace the large hexagon, including a ¼"-wide seam allowance, onto the wrong side of the focus fabric. (For a finished 18"-diameter hexagon, trace an 18½"-diameter shape.) Cut along the traced line.
2. Cut six 1½"-wide strips of facing fabric the length of each side plus 2" to 3".
3. With right sides together, center and sew one facing strip to one hexagon edge, using a ¼"-wide seam allowance. Center and sew a second facing strip to an adjacent side. Working in a

clockwise direction, continue sewing facing strips to the remaining sides of the hexagon.

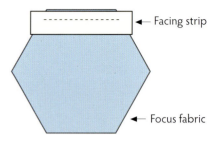

Facing strip

Focus fabric

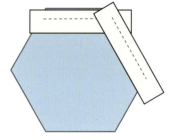

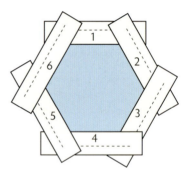

4. Flip the hexagon over so the wrong side of the focus fabric is facing up. Using the edge of the hexagon as a guide, trim the ends of the strips even with the hexagon.

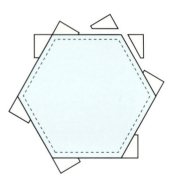

5. Press the facing to the wrong side of the focus fabric, favoring it slightly (see "Favoring"). The shape is now ready for appliqué. The raw edges of each facing strip will be concealed once the shape is appliquéd.

For *reverse appliqué,* focus fabric is placed *behind* a window formed in the background fabric. In this method, the faced shape is created from the background fabric, rather than the hexagon fabric.

1. Trace a hexagon on the wrong side of the facing fabric. Layer the facing fabric and background fabric, right sides together, and pin in place. Sewing on the marked line, stitch completely around the hexagon.

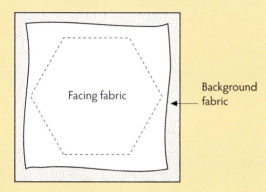

Facing fabric

Background fabric

2. Cut away the center of the hexagon through both layers of fabric, making sure to cut parallel to the stitched line and leaving ¼" for seam allowances. Clip into each corner. This will allow the seam allowances to be pressed flat once the facing is turned to the wrong side of the background fabric.

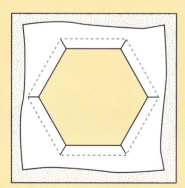

3. Push the facing fabric through the hexagon opening and press it neatly to the wrong side of the background fabric. Referring to "Favoring" (page 8), favor the facing slightly, so the facing does not show on the front of the piece. You can use starch to hold the facing in place, if needed.

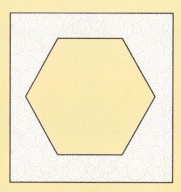

Fold facing to wrong side.

4. Position the focus fabric behind the window and pin in place. Edgestitch around the window to secure the layers. Trim the focus fabric underneath the background fabric, leaving a ¼"-wide seam allowance.

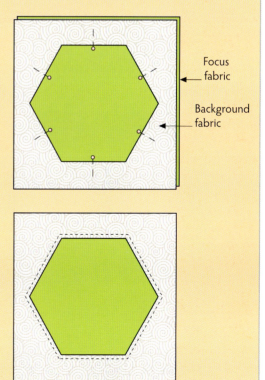

Focus fabric

Background fabric

Joining Hexagons

In addition to constructing faced hexagons with machine appliqué, you can join your hexagons using another simple technique. Use this method for reversible projects, and once the blocks are joined, the piece is finished! You can also join small hexagons to make a large hexagon that can be appliquéd to the background fabric.

Before joining the hexagons, you should first decide the layout of the blocks and arrange them accordingly.

1. Butt the finished edges of two hexagons together, side by side. You may need to rotate a hexagon so that the two touching sides are exactly the same length. Slight irregularities can occur when the facing is stitched to the focus fabric, but the two hexagons should butt up next to each other without overlapping.

2. Use a zigzag or decorative stitch to sew over each of the finished edges as shown. Set the zigzag stitch to medium length and wide enough to span both adjoining pieces. If you don't want to draw attention to the zigzag, reduce the stitch width. For projects with multiple fabric colors, try using gray thread, as it will blend into many of the shades without being too distracting. For the best results, match the thread color to the project when possible. Repeat the process, making a row of hexagons.

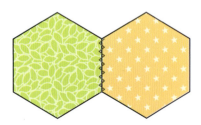

3. To join more than one row, butt the rows next to each other. Stitch the hexagons together as described in step 2, turning the project 60° at the corners as needed.

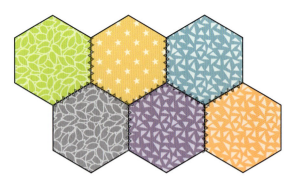

Quilting and Finishing

I recommend machine quilting the appliqué projects in this book. There are at least six layers of fabric, plus batting, along the outer edge of each shape. Sewing through all that bulk by hand would be very difficult. For machine quilting, use a size 90/14 needle to help pierce the layers of fabric.

For appliquéd-hexagon projects, consider skipping the actual appliqué step. (Yes, you read that right.) Plan your appliqué design and pin the shapes in place using a generous number of pins so that the hexagons can't shift. The quilting stitches will double as the appliqué stitches when you free-motion quilt or edgestitch around each shape. The project will finish quickly, though it may take some practice to master combining the steps.

Quilting Motifs

Quilting motifs for such a bold geometric design can prove challenging. There are a few schools of thought on the process. You can echo (or mimic) the hexagon shape, or go for something totally opposite to play counterpoint to the geometric shapes in the quilt.

Opposites. When the quilt looks angular and hard, try quilting it with a soft organic design. Opposites are often appealing. (See "Hexagon Garden" on page 51).

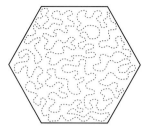

Filler. Filler designs are often quilted from edge to edge across the quilt surface, and generally don't follow the actual details of the blocks or hexagons in the quilt. Fillers can be angular or organic. (See "Honeycomb Hexagons" on page 44.)

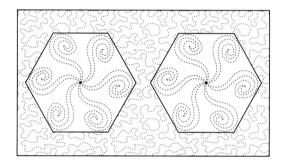

Echo. Echo quilting traces around the primary shapes in the blocks or hexagons to form echoed stitching lines. Using echo quilting ensures that your quilting will match your sharp hexagon design.

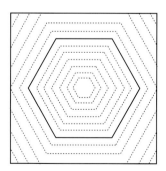

Custom. Custom quilting is a mix of angular, repeated hexagons mixed with organic fill shapes, and is done completely at your discretion. (See "Cascading Hexagons" on page 54.)

Copy the hexagon planning sheet (page 16) and use it to draw your quilting design before stitching on your quilt. The hexagon is divided into six equal portions to give you guidelines and allow you to plan radial effects.

On pages 17–20, you'll find 16 quilting ideas to get you started. Each was drafted using the hexagon planning sheet.

Binding

Binding a quilt with a traditional, hexagon-shaped edge would be the kind of thing that keeps a novice quilter up at night. Thankfully, using the reversible method, all the projects and quilts made with hexagon-shaped edges are already finished and therefore don't require binding. However, I recommend edgestitching around the perimeter of the entire project for added stability.

To bind the straight edges on the appliquéd quilts, use traditional double-fold, continuous binding. For help with applying binding, go to ShopMartingale.com/HowtoQuilt for free downloadable information.

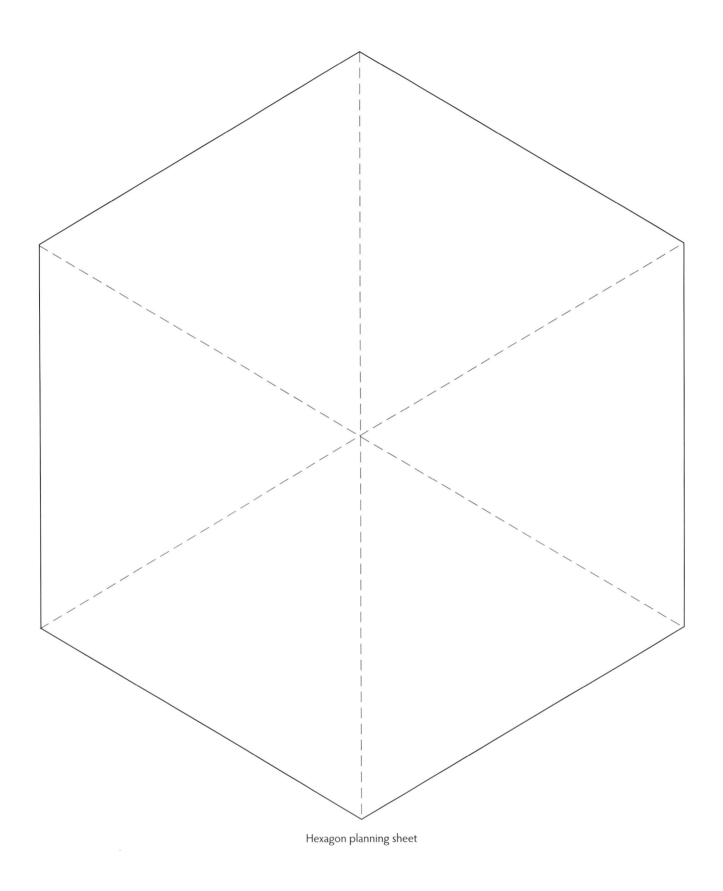

Hexagon planning sheet

Palace Entrance Radial

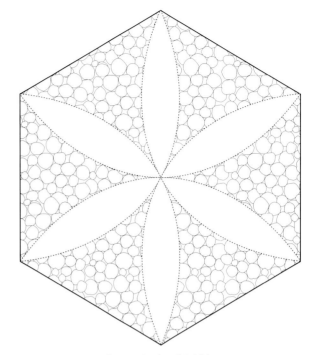

Orange Peel and Pebbles

Shockwave

Feather FIll

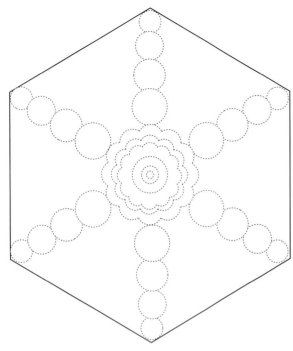

Flower and Pinballs

Hearty Feathers

Radial Swirl

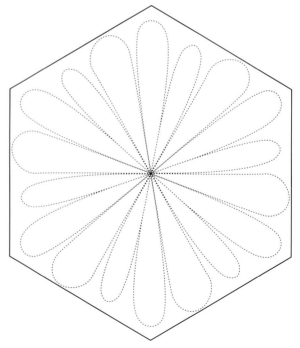

18-Petal Flower

Swirled Flower

Stacked Flower

Echo Fill

Radial Fill Loops

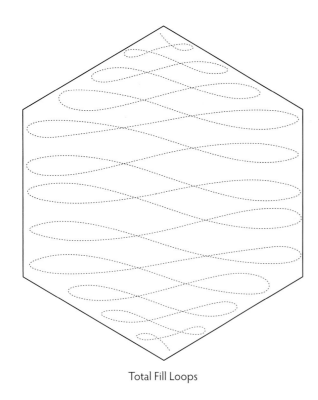

Total Fill Loops

Maze

Mum

Spider Web

the blocks

This chapter contains lots of block ideas for appliquéd hexagons. You can use just one, make repeat blocks, or mix and match for a variety of projects.

The finished size of all the blocks is 15" x 15". While quilt blocks traditionally measure anywhere from 3" to 14" square, I like to make big blocks to save time and money. For a 15" block, you'll need to cut the background fabric 15½" x 15½" to account for seam allowances.

Making the blocks a standard 15" x 15" allows for larger finished projects with less time spent piecing. Table runners are wider, throw pillows are fluffier, and nine-block baby quilts are more snuggly. Having said that, you always have the option to scale down the block designs to finish 12" x 12" if you are more comfortable with that size or are mixing these blocks with other traditional blocks.

The block patterns start on page 23, but first, let's talk about how you can use them to make projects you'll love.

Types of Blocks

You can make four basic types of blocks using the faced-hexagon method.

Single appliquéd. One single-faced shape is applied to a block in various sizes and positions. (See blocks 1, 2, 3, 11, 12, and 13.)

Stacked and appliquéd. Multiple hexagons are applied on top of each other, either centered or off centered. (See blocks 4, 5, 6, 10, 14, 16, 17, and 18.)

Pieced. A hexagon is applied to a background, then sliced and stitched together to form a new design. (See blocks 7, 8 and 17.)

Joined and appliquéd. Hexagons are joined and then appliquéd to a background as a group, similar to how a traditional Grandmother's Flower Garden quilt is made. (See blocks 9 and 15.)

Make It Your Own

By itself, each block design would make an interesting quilt. There are several ways to make a unique and unified quilt with just one repeated block or an assortment of blocks:

Consistent Background Color, Changing Hexagon Color

Use a consistent background color, while changing the hexagon colors. A great way to get a mix of coordinating hexagon colors is to use a pack of precut 5" or 10" squares or a fat-quarter bundle for your focus fabrics.

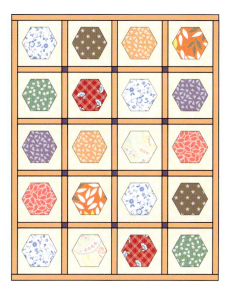

Another option is to use the same focus fabric in each hexagon and change each block's background fabric. In this quilt, the partial hexagon (block 7 on page 28) is white and the background fabric changes in each block.

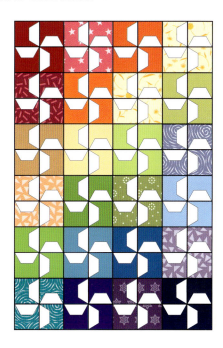

High Contrast, Negative and Positive Spaces

Play with high contrast, switching the positive and negative space in the blocks you are using. You'll often see this method used in monochromatic quilt designs.

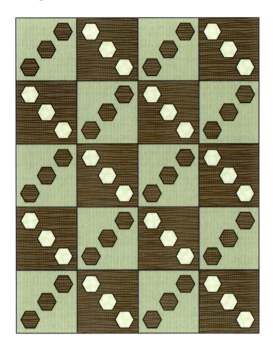

Same Block, Different Rotations

Use the same block design, but rotate alternate blocks 90° when arranging the quilt on your design wall. Blocks that are asymmetrical will work best for this method. An example of this quilt design is shown on page 38.

Different Block Designs

Another way to use these blocks is to design a quilt that uses two or more different blocks. Use a unifying color throughout to create visual interest.

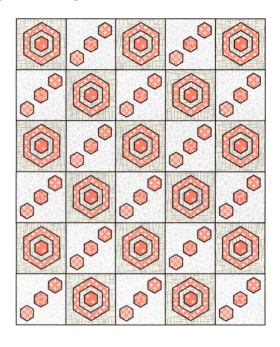

Wild and Scrappy

Lastly, consider making all the blocks in every fabric you own. Make a wild, haphazard cross section of blocks to represent your fabric stash, your interests, your favorite fabric designer, and so on. A quilt made from many different blocks is called a sampler quilt. Samplers often have a scrappy look to them, as they were often made one block at a time when time and fabric allowed. Made with these blocks, samplers will be cohesive by focusing on the hexagon shape and using the same background fabric in each block (see page 38).

How Many Blocks Do I Need?

For each block design, I've provided the fabric requirements, hexagon sizes, and the method used to make one block. Use the chart below to decide how many total 15" blocks you'll need for your project size. For all of these designs, prepare the hexagons as described in "Appliquéd Hexagons" (page 12).

Blocks Needed Per Project							
	Pillow	Runner	Baby	Lap	Twin	Queen	King
Blocks	1	4	9	16	30	42	49
Layout	1 x 1	1 x 4	3 x 3	4 x 4	5 x 6	6 x 7	7 x 7
Finished size	15" x 15"	15" x 60"	45" x 45"	60" x 60"	75" x 90"	90" x 105"	105" x 105"

BLOCK 1 ⬡ Single 12"-Diameter Hexagon

Materials

- 1 square, 15½" x 15½", of fabric for background (Tula Pink for FreeSpirit Fabrics)
- 1 square, 13" x 13", of fabric for hexagon (Art Gallery Fabrics)
- 1 square, 13" x 13", of fabric for facing

Instructions

Make one 12"-diameter hexagon. Center the finished hexagon on the background fabric, making sure two of the hexagon edges are parallel to the edges of the square. Pin in place and then appliqué the hexagon to the background fabric.

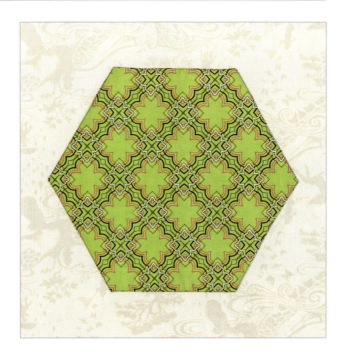

BLOCK 2 ⬡ Three Spaced Hexagons

Materials

- 1 square, 15½" x 15½", of fabric for background (Tula Pink for FreeSpirit Fabrics)
- 3 squares, 5" x 5", of fabric for hexagons (Tula Pink for FreeSpirit Fabrics)
- 3 squares, 5" x 5", of fabric for facing

Instructions

Make three 4½"-diameter hexagons. Fold the background square in half and lightly press a crease along the fold line. Using only half of the background square, center the three hexagons vertically, placing them 1" apart from each other. Pin in place and then appliqué the hexagons to the background fabric.

Materials

- 1 square, 15½" x 15½", of fabric for background (Tula Pink for FreeSpirit Fabrics)
- 1 square, 6" x 6", of fabric for hexagon (Laura Gunn for Michael Miller Fabrics)
- 1 square, 6" x 6", of fabric for facing

Instructions

Make one 5"-diameter hexagon. Fold the background square in half vertically and horizontally. Lightly press a crease along both fold lines. Center the hexagon in one quadrant of the square. Pin in place and then appliqué the hexagon to the background fabric.

Materials

- 1 square, 15½" x 15½", of fabric for background (Tula Pink for FreeSpirit Fabrics)
- 1 square, 13" x 13", of fabric for large hexagon (Kaffe Fasset for Rowan Fabric)
- 1 square, 9" x 9", of fabric for medium hexagon (Kaffe Fasset for Rowan Fabric)
- 1 square, 5" x 5", of fabric for small hexagon (Kaffe Fasset for Rowan Fabric)
- 1 square, 13" x 13", of fabric for facing
- 1 square, 9" x 9", of fabric for facing
- 1 square, 5" x 5", of fabric for facing

Instructions

1. Make one 12"-diameter hexagon, one 7½"-diameter hexagon, and one 4½"-diameter hexagon. Place the small hexagon on top of the medium hexagon, off centered by any amount. In the sample, the small hexagon is placed ¾" from each edge in one corner of the medium hexagon. Pin in place and then appliqué the small hexagon to the medium hexagon.
2. Carefully cut away the excess fabric from underneath the small hexagon to reduce bulk in the final block.
3. Place the stacked unit on top of the large hexagon, off centered the same amount as before (in this case ¾" from each edge). Pin in place and then appliqué the stacked unit to the large hexagon. Carefully cut away the excess fabric from underneath the medium hexagon.
4. Center the stacked hexagon unit on the background square. Make sure two of the hexagon's edges are parallel to the edges of the square. Pin in place and then appliqué the unit to the background fabric.

Materials

- 1 square, 15½" x 15½", of fabric for background (Tula Pink for FreeSpirit Fabrics)
- 1 square, 13" x 13", of fabric for large hexagon (Tula Pink for FreeSpirit Fabrics)
- 1 square, 9" x 9", of fabric for medium hexagon (Tula Pink for FreeSpirit Fabrics)
- 1 square, 5" x 5", of fabric for small hexagon (Kate Spain for Moda Fabrics)
- 1 square, 13" x 13", of fabric for facing
- 1 square, 9" x 9", of fabric for facing
- 1 square, 5" x 5", of fabric for facing

Instructions

1. Make one 12"-diameter hexagon, one 7½"-diameter hexagon, and one 4½"-diameter hexagon. Center the small hexagon on top of the medium hexagon. Pin in place and then appliqué the small hexagon to the medium hexagon.
2. Carefully cut away the excess fabric from underneath the small hexagon to reduce bulk in the final block.
3. Center the stacked unit on top of the large hexagon and pin in place. Appliqué the stacked unit to the large hexagon. Carefully cut away the excess fabric from underneath the medium hexagon.
4. Center the stacked hexagon unit on the background square. Make sure two of the hexagon's edges are parallel to the edges of the square. Pin in place and then appliqué the unit to the background fabric.

⬡ transparency

The transparency in this block is achieved by making the medium hexagon from the block background fabric. You can also achieve this look by creating a window in the large hexagon using the "Window Design" method (page 13). Center the large hexagon on the background square and appliqué in place. Then center the small hexagon in the window and appliqué it to the background fabric. If using this method, you will not need the medium hexagon.

Materials

- 1 square, 15½" x 15½", of fabric for background (Tula Pink for FreeSpirit Fabrics)
- 1 square, 13" x 13", of fabric for large hexagon (Anna Maria Horner for FreeSpirit Fabrics)
- 2 squares, 3" x 3", of fabric for small hexagons (Anna Maria Horner for FreeSpirit Fabrics)
- 1 square, 13" x 13", of fabric for facing
- 2 squares, 3" x 3", of fabric for facing

Instructions

1. Make one 12"-diameter hexagon and two 2½"-diameter hexagons. Evenly space the small hexagons along one edge of the large hexagon. When you are pleased with the arrangement, pin them in place and then appliqué the small hexagons to the large hexagon.
2. Carefully cut away the excess fabric from underneath the small hexagons to reduce bulk in the final block.
3. Center the large hexagon on the background square. Pin in place and then appliqué the hexagon to the background fabric.

Materials

- 4 squares, 8" x 8", of fabric for background (Tula Pink for FreeSpirit Fabrics)
- 2 squares, 9" x 9", of fabric for hexagons (Anna Maria Horner for FreeSpirit Fabrics)
- 2 squares, 9" x 9", of fabric for facing

Instructions

1. Make two 7½"-diameter hexagons. For block 7, cut each hexagon in half diagonally from corner to corner to make four half hexagons. For block 8, mark the midpoint on one straight side and on the opposite straight side of each hexagon; then cut from mark to mark to make four half hexagons.

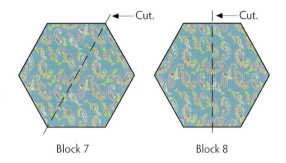

Block 7   Block 8

2. Position a half hexagon on each background square, aligning the raw edges and leaving ¼" for seam allowances on each end as shown. This will allow the half hexagons to meet in the center without sewing through the hexagon. Pin in place and then appliqué a half hexagon to each background square.

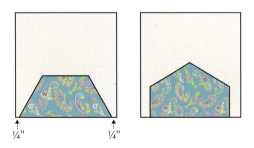

3. Lay out the four appliquéd background squares, rotating the squares 90° to create a pinwheel. Sew the squares together in pairs. Press the seam allowances open.

4. Join the pairs, matching the center seam intersections. Press the seam allowances open.

BLOCK 9 ⬡ Hexagon Flower

Materials

- 1 square, 15½" x 15½", of fabric for background (Tula Pink for FreeSpirit Fabrics)
- 7 squares, 5" x 5", of fabric for hexagons (Art Gallery Fabrics)
- 7 squares, 5" x 5", of fabric for facing

Instructions

Make seven 4½"-diameter hexagons. Butt the seven hexagons next to each other to form a flower shape. Referring to "Joining Hexagons" (page 14), use a decorative stitch to join the pieces. Gently press. Center the flower on the background square and pin in place. Appliqué the flower to the background fabric.

BLOCK 10 ⬡ Two Stacked Hexagons

Materials

- 1 square, 15½" x 15½", fabric for background (Tula Pink for FreeSpirit Fabrics)
- 1 square, 13" x 13", of fabric for large hexagon (Denyse Schmidt for Jo-Ann Fabrics)
- 1 square, 5" x 5", of fabric for small hexagon (Denyse Schmidt for Jo-Ann Fabrics)
- 1 square, 13" x 13", of fabric for facing
- 1 square, 5" x 5", of fabric for facing

Instructions

1. Make one 12"-diameter hexagon and one 4½"-diameter hexagon. Place the small hexagon 1½" from each edge in one corner of the large hexagon. Pin in place and then appliqué the small hexagon to the large hexagon.
2. Carefully cut away the excess fabric from underneath the small hexagon to reduce bulk in the final block.
3. Center the large hexagon on the background square. Pin in place and then appliqué the hexagon to the background fabric.

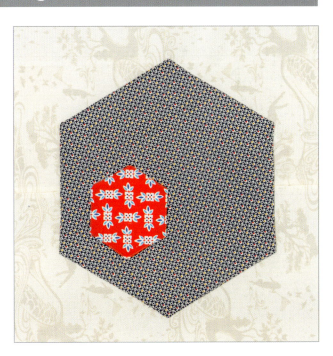

BLOCK 11 ◆ Corner Medium Hexagon

Materials

- 1 square, 15½" x 15½", of fabric for background (Tula Pink for FreeSpirit Fabrics)
- 1 square, 10" x 10", of fabric for hexagon (Kona Solids by Robert Kaufman Fabrics)
- 1 square, 10" x 10", of fabric for facing

Instructions

Make one 9"-diameter hexagon. Place the hexagon in one corner of the background square, 1" from both raw edges. Pin in place and then appliqué the hexagon to the background fabric.

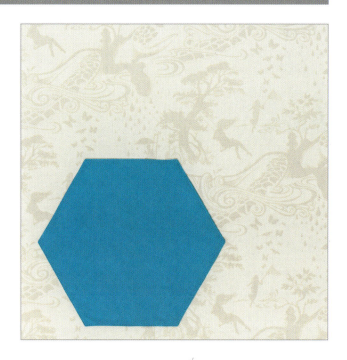

BLOCK 12 ◆ Three Diagonal Hexagons

Materials

- 1 square, 15½" x 15½", of fabric for background (Tula Pink for FreeSpirit Fabrics)
- 3 squares, 5" x 5", of fabric for hexagons (Denyse Schmidt for Jo-Ann Fabrics)
- 3 squares, 5" x 5", of fabric for facing

Instructions

1. Make three 4½"-diameter hexagons. Fold the background square in half diagonally in both directions and lightly crease to find the center of the square. Place the first hexagon in the center of the square, aligning the diagonal points on the hexagon with one of the creased lines. Pin in place and then appliqué the hexagon to the background fabric.
2. Place the two remaining hexagons along the creased diagonal line, spacing them 1½" from the points of the center hexagon. Pin in place and then appliqué the hexagons to the background fabric.

BLOCK 13 ⬡ Three Vertical Hexagons

Materials

- 1 square, 15½" x 15½", of fabric for background (Tula Pink for FreeSpirit Fabrics)
- 3 squares, 5" x 5", of fabric for hexagons (Denyse Schmidt for Jo-Ann Fabrics)
- 3 squares, 5" x 5", of fabric for facing

Instructions

1. Make three 4½"-diameter hexagons. Fold the background square in half vertically and horizontally. Lightly crease to mark the center of the square. Place the first hexagon in the center of the square, aligning the diagonal points on the hexagon with the horizontal creased line. Pin in place and then appliqué the hexagon to the background fabric.

2. Place the two remaining hexagons along the creased vertical line, spacing them ¾" from the center hexagon. One straight side should be parallel to a straight side on the center hexagon as shown in the photo. Pin in place and then appliqué the hexagons to the background fabric.

Materials

- 1 square, 15½" x 15½", of fabric for background (Tula Pink for FreeSpirit Fabrics)
- 1 square, 10" x 10", of fabric for large hexagon (Art Gallery Fabrics)
- 1 square, 8" x 8", of fabric for medium hexagon (Art Gallery Fabrics)
- 1 square, 6" x 6", of fabric for small hexagon (Art Gallery Fabrics)
- 1 square, 10" x 10", of fabric for facing
- 1 square, 8" x 8", of fabric for facing
- 1 square, 6" x 6", of fabric for facing

Instructions

Make one 9"-diameter hexagon, one 7½"-diameter hexagon, and one 5"-diameter hexagon. Fold the background square in half vertically and lightly press a crease along the fold line. Evenly space the hexagons on the creased line, placing a point of each hexagon on the creased line. The large and small hexagons should be 1" from the raw edges of the background square. Pin in place. Appliqué the large hexagon to the background square, folding the other two hexagons out of the way so you can appliqué around the entire shape. Then, fold the small hexagon out of the way and appliqué the medium hexagon in place. Lastly, appliqué the small hexagon in place.

⬡ design variation

For a festive design variation, make hexagons in shades of white and appliqué them in a vertical row. Then embellish with buttons to make a Snowman block. See the quilt idea on page 38.

BLOCK 15 ⬡ Hexagon Ring

Materials

- 1 square, 15½" x 15½", of fabric for background (Tula Pink for FreeSpirit Fabrics)
- 12 squares, 3" x 3", of fabric for hexagons (Kona Solids by Robert Kaufman Fabrics)
- 12 squares, 3" x 3", of fabric for facing

Instructions

1. Make 12 hexagons, 2½" diameter. Arrange the hexagons in a ring. The sample shown uses the color wheel for placement inspiration. When you are pleased with the arrangement, use a zigzag stitch to join the pieces to create the ring. Refer to "Joining Hexagons" (page 14) as needed. Gently press.

2. Fold the background square in half vertically and horizontally, lightly creasing to establish centering lines. Center the hexagon ring on the background square and pin in place. Appliqué the ring to the background square.

Materials

- 1 square, 15½" x 15½", of fabric for background (Tula Pink for FreeSpirit Fabrics)
- 1 square, 9" x 9", of fabric for hexagon (Moda Fabrics)
- 1 square, 8" x 8", of fabric for hexagon (Benartex Fabrics)
- 1 square, 7" x 7", of fabric for hexagon (Benartex Fabrics)
- 1 square, 5" x 5", of fabric for hexagon (Benartex Fabrics)
- 1 square, 9" x 9", of fabric for facing
- 1 square, 8" x 8", of fabric for facing
- 1 square, 7" x 7", of fabric for facing
- 1 square, 5" x 5", of fabric for facing

Instructions

This tossed design was inspired by "Cascading Hexagons" (page 54). You can use any variety and quantity of hexagon sizes.

Make one 8½"-diameter hexagon, one 7½"-diameter hexagon, one 6½"-diameter hexagon, and one 4"-diameter hexagon. Randomly place the hexagons in the center of the background square, allowing the shapes to tilt and overlap. Pin in place. Appliqué the hexagons to the background square starting with the bottom layer. If one hexagon is positioned on top of another hexagon, fold the top hexagon out of the way so you can appliqué around the entire shape of the bottom appliqué.

Materials

- 1 square, 15½" x 15½", of fabric for background (Tula Pink for FreeSpirit Fabrics)
- 1 rectangle, 9" x 16", of fabric for half hexagon (Tokyo Rocco by Carol Van Zandt for Andover Fabrics)
- 1 square, 6½" x 6½", of fabric for small hexagon (Tokyo Rocco by Carol Van Zandt for Andover Fabrics)
- 3 strips, 1½" x 10", of fabric for facing
- 1 square, 6½" x 6½", of fabric for facing

Instructions

You can make a whole 15"-diameter hexagon and cut it in half, using both pieces on two different blocks, or you can simply use the rectangle to create a half hexagon, cut from corner to corner. The following instructions are for making a half hexagon.

1. Make one 15"-diameter half hexagon using the strip facing method described in "Facing Large Hexagons" (page 12). Make one 5¾"-diameter hexagon.

2. Align the half hexagon along one edge of the background square, leaving ¼" at each end for seam allowances. Pin in place and then appliqué the half hexagon to the background fabric.

3. Place the small hexagon in the center of the background square, overlapping the half hexagon as shown in the photo. Pin in place and then appliqué the hexagon to the background fabric.

Materials

- 1 square, 15½" x 15½", of fabric for background (Tula Pink for FreeSpirit Fabrics)
- 4 squares, 5" x 5", of fabric for hexagons (Benartex Fabrics)
- 4 squares, 5" x 5", of fabric for facing

Instructions

Make four 4"-diameter hexagons. In one corner of the background square, arrange the hexagons in a quarter-circle arc. The hexagons at each end of the arc should be ¼" from the raw edge of the square to allow for seam allowances. A hexagon corner should point to the midpoint along the edge of the square. Allow the hexagons to overlap as they tilt around the arc. Pin in place and then appliqué the hexagon to the background fabric.

⬡ creating a perfect circle

By aligning the hexagons at the square's exact midpoint when creating the arc, it will allow you to create a full circle if you want to join this block to other identical blocks. See the quilt idea on page 39.

block-based quilt ideas

In this section, you'll find a few examples showing how to turn blocks into interesting quilts. With so many blocks to work with, the ideas are almost endless.

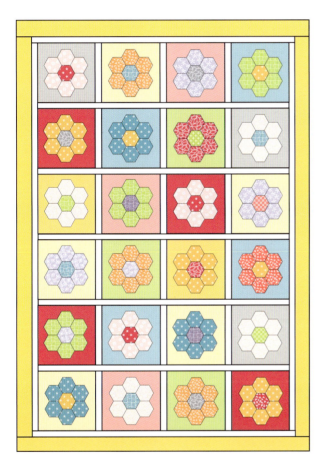

This design features block 9 (page 29), using a coordinating fabric collection. Instead of choosing one fabric for the hexagons or the background, I've mixed all the elements, letting the recognizable flower shape be the focus of the quilt. A yellow border and white sashing have been added to break up the quilt's random scrappiness.

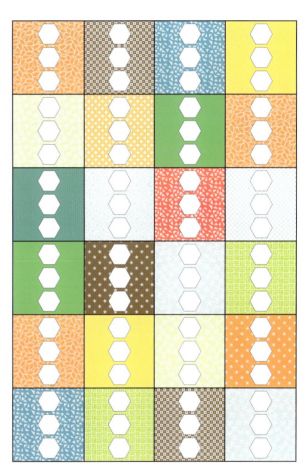

This quilt features only block 13 (page 31). You can use a fat-quarter bundle to make a scrappy-looking background while the white hexgons form consistent vertical stripes.

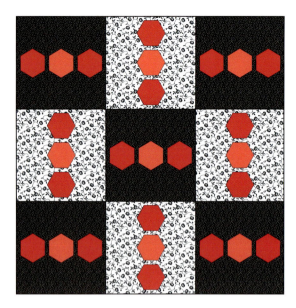

Block 13 (page 31) was also used to create this quilt design with rotated blocks to add visual interest. The background fabrics alternate between black and white, while the constant red hexagons unify the quilt.

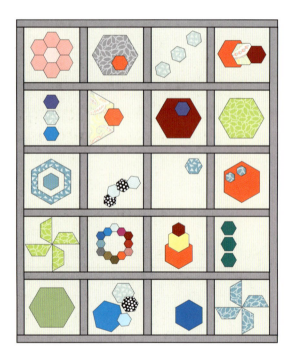

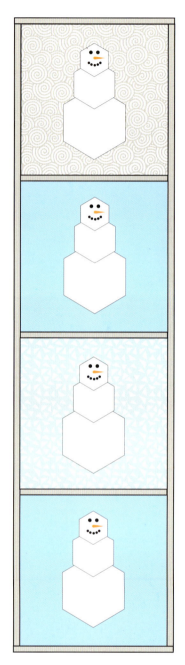

To create a sampler quilt that really works, make as many blocks as you need for your desired size. In this quilt, one background fabric was used throughout, unifying the quilt while still showcasing a variety of block designs. The sashing and borders were made from gray solids to complement the variety of colors in the focus fabrics.

This festive snowman wall hanging was made from only one hexagon block. The usual layout for a table runner (one row of four blocks) has been turned vertically to create these winter friends. Each snowman, made from block 14 (page 32), has buttons for his eyes and mouth and a scrap of orange fabric for his nose.

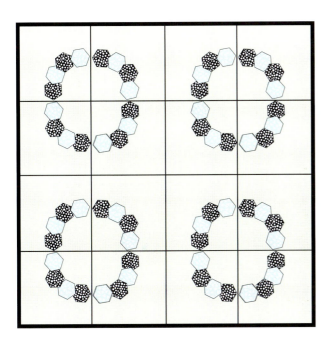

Since some blocks are directional, consider rotating them to form secondary shapes. This design has four rows of four blocks each, rotating block 18 (page 36) to create a circular effect.

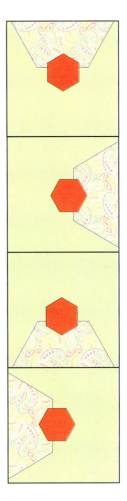

This unique table runner is made from block 17 (page 35) rotated 90°. The effect is a funky, one-of-a-kind look.

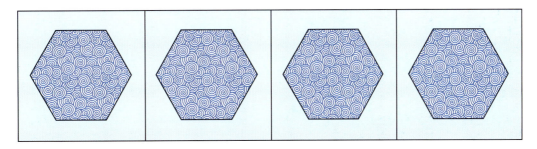

In this table runner, block 1 (page 23) is repeated to give a more traditional feeling to a modern block design.

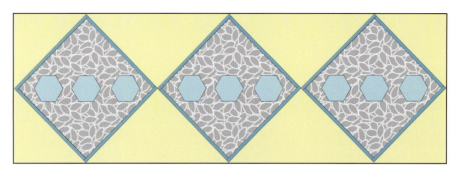

Instead of four blocks, this table runner requires only three of block 12 (page 30) set on point. Narrow sashing and setting triangles are added using traditional quilt-assembly methods.

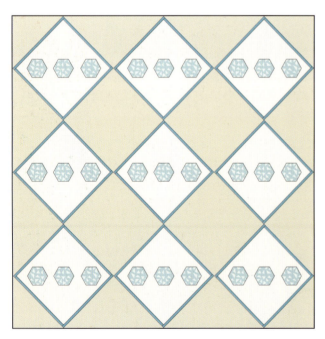

This lap-sized design is based on the table runner above. The on-point design is simply repeated using nine hexagon blocks and four plain blocks.

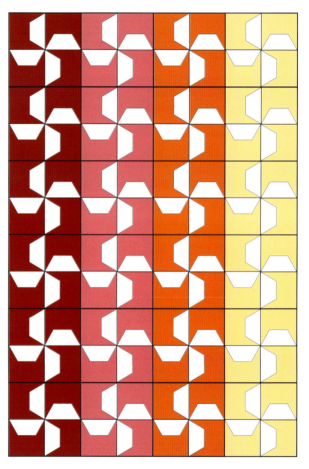

Consider repeating any table-runner design to create a quilt with color-blocked vertical stripes. This quilt requires 24 of block 7 (page 28), or six total rows of the table-runner version on page 67.

Whole-Cloth Quilts and Coverlets

In a whole-cloth quilt, the top is made from one fabric, often without piecing, and normally showcases intricate quilting designs.

For the purposes of this book, I use the term *whole cloth* loosely as we explore geometric shapes appliquéd on a whole piece of background fabric. You can substitute 100% cotton flat bed sheets for the background yardage, since they're already bed sized and seamless. Or, you can use 108"-wide fabric for larger designs and 42"-wide fabric for smaller designs, such as baby quilts and wall hangings.

These appliquéd quilts are heavy. This may seem like a strange thing to note, but depending on whether or not you choose to remove the facing fabric and/or the background fabric from behind the appliquéd shapes, each quilt may have three layers of fabric on the top, plus batting and backing under each shape. Consider the weight of the quilt top when choosing its batting and end use.

A coverlet is a blanket or cover that lacks the three traditional quilt layers (top, batting, and backing) and does not have a quilting design over the entire project.

The two coverlet projects in this book are constructed in the same fashion: a lap-sized and a doll-sized coverlet (suitable for 18" dolls). You can adjust the size of a coverlet simply by adding or subtracting hexagons as needed, or by increasing or decreasing the size of the hexagons.

Since a coverlet doesn't have a batting layer, you can add warmth by using flannel as the reversible facing fabric.

Once the hexagons are constructed and pressed, they're joined as described on page 14, and the project is finished. The coverlet will have unique-shaped edges that don't require binding.

hexagon circle

This wall hanging with hexagons arranged in a circle is a great starter project for anyone with a beginning skill level. Use the basic radial design to showcase fabric scraps or experiment with color theory.

Finished size: 31" x 31" • **Hexagon size:** 5" diameter • **Skill level:** Beginner

Made and machine quilted by Jen Eskridge.

Materials

Yardage is based on 42"-wide fabric.

- 1 yard of fabric for background
- ¾ yard *total* of assorted fabrics for hexagons (at least 6" x 6") and binding
- ½ yard of fabric for facing
- 1 yard of fabric for backing
- 36" x 36" piece of batting

Fabrics: Anna Marie Horner for FreeSpirit Fabrics

Cutting

From the background fabric, cut:
1 square, 31" x 31"

From the assorted fabrics, cut *a total of:*
4 binding strips, 2½" x 42"

Making the Quilt Top

Refer to "Preparing the Facing Hexagons" (page 10) and "Appliquéd Hexagons" (page 12) for detailed instructions as needed.

1. Prepare 12 assorted 5"-diameter hexagons for appliqué.
2. Fold the background square in half vertically and horizontally. Lightly press a crease along each fold line. Then fold the background square diagonally in both directions. Lightly press a crease along each fold line.

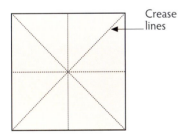

Crease lines

3. Center four hexagons on the vertical and horizontal crease lines, placing them 2½" from the raw edges of the background square. Pin in place.

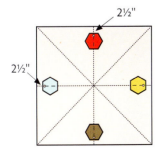

2½"
2½"

4. Place hexagons on both sides of each diagonal crease line to form a circle. The hexagons should be equidistant from each other; adjust as needed and pin in place.

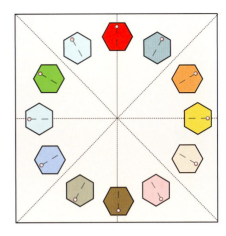

5. Appliqué the hexagons to the background fabric.

Finishing the Quilt

For more information on any finishing techniques, please visit ShopMartingale.com/HowtoQuilt to download free illustrated how-to instructions.

1. Layer the quilt top, batting, and backing; baste the layers together. Quilt as desired.
2. Bind the quilt using the 2½"-wide binding strips, and then add a label.

● designer's note

This quilt is a great design to turn into a large wall clock, simply by adding clock movement hardware from your local craft or hardware store. Or, it would make a nice table centerpiece because you could put a candle, centerpiece, or platter in the middle without obstructing the hexagon design.

honeycomb hexagons

Showcase your favorite fabric line with these assorted hexagons, or use themed prints to make an I-spy baby quilt.

Finished size: 40" x 60" ● **Hexagon size:** 8½" diameter ● **Skill level:** Intermediate

Made and machine quilted by Jen Eskridge.

Materials

Yardage is based on 42"-wide fabric.

- 1¾ yards of fabric for background
- 40 squares, 10" x 10", of assorted fabrics for hexagons
- 2⅜ yards of fabric for facing
- ½ yard of fabric for binding
- 2 yards of fabric for backing
- 45" x 65" piece of batting

Fabrics: Just Wing It precut 10" squares from MoMo by Moda

Cutting

From the background fabric, cut:
1 rectangle, 40" x 60"

From the binding fabric, cut:
4 strips, 2½" x 42"

Making the Quilt Top

Refer to "Preparing the Facing Hexagons" (page 10) and "Appliquéd Hexagons" (page 12) for detailed instructions as needed.

1. Prepare 33 assorted 8½"-diameter hexagons for appliqué. Set aside the leftover 10" squares to make the backing.
2. Fold the background rectangle in half vertically and horizontally. Lightly press a crease along the fold lines to find the center of the rectangle.
3. Place the first hexagon in the exact center position, making sure two hexagon points line up with the horizontal crease.

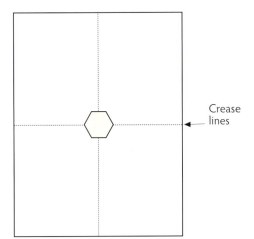

Crease lines

4. Arrange and pin the remaining hexagons on the background in five vertical rows, leaving a consistent ¾" to 1" space between each hexagon. This will create a sashing effect.

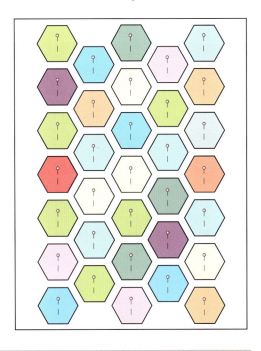

⬡ see it

I recommend laying out the quilt on a design wall or other large, flat surface in your workspace. If you're using a larger background piece, such as a sheet, you can make the design bigger by leaving larger spaces between each shape.

5. Appliqué the hexagons in place, or you can appliqué them during the quilting process. The sample quilt shown on the facing page was made by combining the appliqué and quilting in one step as described in "Quilting and Finishing" (page 14).

Finishing the Quilt

For more information on any finishing techniques, please visit ShopMartingale.com/HowtoQuilt to download free illustrated how-to instructions.

1. To make the backing, cut the piece of backing fabric lengthwise (parallel to the selvage edge) to make two 72"-long pieces. Join the seven leftover 10" squares to make a row. Sew a backing piece on each side of the pieced row. Press the seam allowances open and trim the backing pieces even with the pieced row. The backing should measure at least 45" x 65".

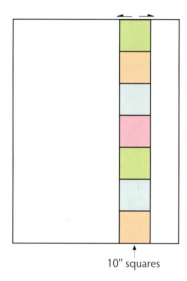

10" squares

Quilting ideas

2. Layer the quilt top, batting, and backing; baste the layers together. Quilt as desired.
3. Bind the quilt using the 2½"-wide binding strips, and then add a label.

hexagon rows

In this quilt you'll join the hexagons to make a row and then appliqué the entire row to the background. It's a speedy quilt with interesting composition.

Finished size: 50" x 62" ● **Hexagon size:** 9" diameter ● **Skill level:** Intermediate
Made by Jen Eskridge and machine quilted by Colleen Eskridge.

Materials

Yardage is based on 42"-wide fabric. Fat quarters measure 18" x 21".

- 1⅝ yards of green solid for background
- 4 or 5 fat quarters of assorted black-on-white prints for hexagons
- 4 or 5 fat quarters of assorted white-on-black prints for hexagons
- ⅞ yard of black-and-white floral for border
- 2⅓ yards of fabric for facing
- ⅝ yard of fabric for binding
- 3¼ yards of fabric for backing
- 56" x 69" piece of batting

Fabrics: Essentials II by Studio E Fabrics and Kona Solids by Robert Kaufman Fabrics

Cutting

From the green solid, cut:*
1 rectangle, 42" x 54"

From the black-and-white floral, cut:
6 strips, 4½" x 42"

From the binding fabric, cut:
7 strips, 2½" x 42"

*For this project, you can use the full width of your fabric, which may be 42" or even a bit wider.

Making the Quilt Top

Refer to "Preparing the Facing Hexagons" (page 10) and "Appliquéd Hexagons" (page 12) for detailed instructions as needed.

1. Prepare 15 black-on-white and 15 white-on-black 9"-diameter hexagons for appliqué.
2. Using a narrow zigzag stitch, join five black-on-white hexagons to make a row as described in "Joining Hexagons" (page 14). Repeat to make a total of three rows of black-on-white hexagons.

Make 3.

3. Repeat step 2, using the white-on-black hexagons to make three rows.
4. Sew black-and-white floral strips to the short ends of the green rectangle. Join the remaining four floral strips end to end. From the long strip, cut two 62"-long strips. Sew them to the remaining two sides of the green rectangle. Press the seam allowances toward the floral strips.

5. Position the hexagon rows on the green rectangle. Make sure each row is centered from left to right and the rows are equidistant from each other. Securely pin the rows in place.

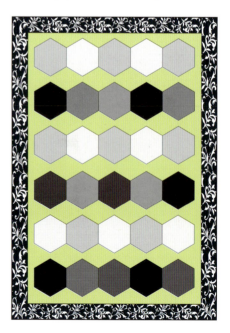

● **designer's note**

The borders are added before the center is appliquéd to give the creative sewist the option of staggering the rows and allowing the hexagons to float beyond the background rectangle.

6. Appliqué the rows to the quilt top. If desired, carefully remove the background fabric from underneath each hexagon row. Use the fabric to make a matching pillow or save it for your scrap stash.

Finishing the Quilt

For more information on any finishing techniques, please visit ShopMartingale.com/HowtoQuilt to download free illustrated how-to instructions.

1. Layer the quilt top, batting, and backing; baste the layers together. Quilt as desired.
2. Bind the quilt using the 2½"-wide binding strips, and then add a label.

Quilting ideas

⬡ make it queen size

Finished size: 84" x 91"

Materials

Yardage is based on 42"-wide fabric. Fat quarters measure 18" x 21".

- 4¼ yards of fabric for background
- 1⅓ yards of fabric for border
- 40 squares, 10" x 10", of assorted prints for hexagons
- 4 or 5 fat quarters of assorted prints for hexagons
- 3½ yards of fabric for facing
- ⅞ yard of fabric for binding
- 7¾ yards of fabric for backing
- 89" x 96" piece of batting

Cutting

From the background fabric, cut:*
2 pieces, 42" x 76"

From the border fabric, cut:
9 strips, 4½" x 42"

From the binding fabric, cut:
10 strips, 2½" x 42"

*For this project, you can use the full width of your fabric, which may be 42" or even a bit wider.

Making the Quilt Top

1. Prepare 56 assorted 9"-diameter hexagons for appliqué.
2. Using a narrow zigzag stitch, join eight assorted hexagons to make a row as described in "Joining Hexagons." Repeat to make a total of seven rows.
3. Trim the selvages from the two background pieces. Then join the pieces along one long edge to make a 76" x 83" rectangle.
4. Join the border strips end to end. From the long strip, cut two 76" long strips and sew them to the short ends of the rectangle. From the remaining long strip, cut two 91"-long strips and sew them to the remaining two sides of the rectangle. Press the seam allowances toward the border strips.
5. Position the hexagon rows on the quilt top as described in step 5 on page 48. Securely pin and then appliqué the rows in place.
6. Finish the quilt as described on page 49.

hexagon garden

This quilt features the graphic element of "Hexagon Rows"
(page 47), with an easy construction method for larger quilts.

Finished size: 80" x 88" ● **Hexagon size:** 17" diameter ● **Skill level:** Intermediate
Made and machine quilted by Karen Morello.

Materials

Yardage is based on 42"-wide fabric.

- 2⅝ yards *each* of 2 cream prints for background
- ½ yard *each* of 10 assorted fabrics for hexagons and facing strips
- ¾ yard *total* of color-coordinated fabric for facing strips
- ⅞ yard of fabric for binding
- 7½ yards of fabric for backing
- 85" x 93" piece of batting

Fabrics: Road to Marrakesh by Studio E Fabrics

⬡ use it up!

Cutting 1½"-wide facing strips from the left-over assorted fabrics will give you the most bang for your quilting buck. However, if you want to save your assorted fabrics for another project, you'll need a total of 1⅜ yards of color-coordinated fabrics for the facing strips.

Cutting

From the *lengthwise grain* of *each* cream print, cut:
2 strips, 20½" x 88" (4 total)

From the binding fabric, cut:
9 strips, 2½" x 42"

Making the Quilt Top

Refer to "Facing Large Hexagons" (page 12) and "Appliquéd Hexagons" (page 12) for detailed instructions as needed.

1. Prepare 20 assorted 17"-diameter hexagons for appliqué, using the strip facing technique.
2. Using a narrow zigzag stitch, join five assorted hexagons to make a row as described in "Joining Hexagons" (page 14). Repeat to make a total of four rows.

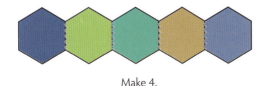

Make 4.

3. Fold each background strip in half vertically and horizontally. Lightly press a crease along the fold lines. Center each hexagon row and pin in place. Use an edgestitch to appliqué each row in place. Press each appliquéd strip.

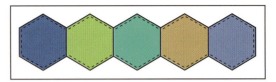

4. Join the four appliquéd strips to complete the quilt, alternating the cream background strips. Press the seam allowances in one direction.

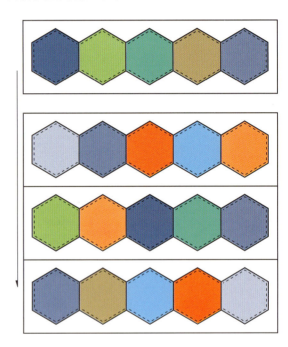

Finishing the Quilt

For more information on any finishing techniques, please visit ShopMartingale.com/HowtoQuilt to download free illustrated how-to instructions.

1. Layer the quilt top, batting, and backing; baste the layers together. Quilt as desired.
2. Bind the quilt using the 2½"-wide binding strips, and then add a label.

Made and machine quilted by Karen Morello, this quilt features assorted pink fat quarters and black-and-white fabrics from Hoffman Fabrics. Appliqué the hexagons and then join the strips, alternating them to create visual interest.

cascading hexagons

Not only is this quilt modern and visually striking, it's also a stash buster when it comes to fabrics. Pick a color from your stash and let that be your guide to this monochromatic gem. See the quilt on page 56 for a more subtle pallet mixed with a truly fresh design.

Finished size: 88" x 97" ● **Hexagon size:** 2" to 24" diameter ● **Skill level:** Advanced

Made by Jen Eskridge and machine quilted by Evelyn Gernaat.

Materials

Yardage is based on 42"-wide fabric.

- 4¼ yards *total* of assorted orange and yellow prints for hexagons*
- 2⅝ yard of 108"-wide gray solid for background
- 4¼ yards of fabric for facing
- ⅞ yard of fabric for binding
- 2⅝ yard of 108"-wide fabric for backing**
- 93" x 102" piece of batting

*The assorted prints should all be from one color family and range in value from dark to light.
**Bust your stash by making the backing from large fabric pieces in the same color family as the quilt front so they will coordinate. You'll need a total of 8 yards of 42"-wide fabric for a quilt back.*

⬡ use a flat sheet

If you can't find 108"-wide fabric in just the right color, you can purchase two queen-size flat bed sheets (one for the background and one for the backing). Wash and press the sheets. Then trim off the hems. The size of your finished quilt will vary depending on the size of the sheets.

Cutting

From the background fabric, cut:
1 piece, 88" x 97"

From the binding fabric, cut:
10 strips, 2½" x 42"

Making the Quilt Top

This quilt design is largely intuitive and will vary with each quilt and its creator. You may choose to use more or fewer hexagons of any given size. The design is completely up to you. Use the listed number and sizes of hexagons as a guide. Generally, you will want more small hexagons and fewer large hexagons. In the quilt on page 54, the colors fade from darker large hexagons on the bottom to lighter small hexagons toward the top. Start by making a few hexagons in each size; then you can make more hexagons from the appropriate fabrics as needed. Refer to "Preparing the Facing Hexagons" (page 10), "Facing Large Hexagons" (page 12), and "Appliquéd Hexagons" (page 12) for detailed instructions as needed.

1. Using the assorted prints, prepare the hexagons for appliqué as follows:
   - 3 hexagons, 24" diameter
   - 5 hexagons, 18" diameter
   - 6 hexagons, 9" diameter
   - 14 hexagons, 5" diameter

2. Place the background fabric on a design wall or other large, flat surface, such as a floor. Arrange the largest hexagons along the bottom edge of the background, tilting and overlapping them slightly. Pin in place.

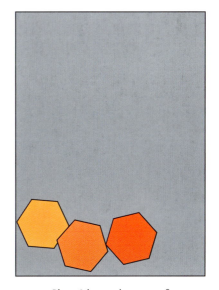

Place 3 largest hexagons first.

3. Along the right side of the background, add the next largest hexagons above the first row of hexagons. Tilt each shape and overlap them slightly to create a flow in the composition.

4. Continue adding hexagons to the right side of the background, working toward the top edge as shown in the photo on page 54. When you are pleased with the arrangement, securely pin the hexagons in place.
5. Carefully move the piece to your sewing machine. Use an edgestitch to appliqué the hexagons in place.

change the foot

If you're comfortable using a free-motion presser foot, you can use it to appliqué the shapes. This foot will allow you to stitch in all directions without having to rotate the background piece under the sewing machine as often.

Finishing the Quilt

For more information on any finishing techniques, please visit ShopMartingale.com/HowtoQuilt to download free illustrated how-to instructions.

1. Layer the quilt top, batting, and backing; baste the layers together. Quilt as desired. There is a large amount of negative space, so plan your quilting designs accordingly.
2. Bind the quilt using the 2½"-wide binding strips, and then add a label.

color option

Made by Jen Eskridge and machine quilted by Evelyn Gernaat, the different values of cream are intermixed on the background of this quilt. It's also quilted differently, which changes the project's feel. Both styles offer a unique look and you may choose to arrange the shapes in any manner.

doll coverlet

Make this coverlet for your little one's best little friend. The possibilities of this reversible project are practically endless—one side can feature the child's favorite colors while the other can feature holiday-themed prints. Plus, it's such a manageable size—why not make several?

Finished size: 20" x 25" • **Hexagon size:** 4½" diameter • **Skill level:** Beginner

Made by Jen Eskridge.

Materials

- 31 squares, 5" x 5", of assorted prints for hexagons
- ½ yard of fabric for facing*

Fabrics: Fresh Flowers by Deb Strain for Moda

Choose a fabric that coordinates with or complements the fabric squares, as this project is completely reversible.

Making the Coverlet

Refer to "Preparing the Facing Hexagons" (page 10) and "Reversible Hexagons" (page 11) for detailed instructions as needed.

1. Prepare 31 assorted 4½"-diameter reversible hexagons.
2. Butt the hexagons next to each other and use a narrow zigzag stitch to join four assorted hexagons into a row as described in "Joining Hexagons" (page 14). Make a total of four rows of four hexagons each. Repeat to make three rows of five hexagons each.
3. Use a narrow zigzag stitch to join the rows, pivoting the piece 60° at each corner, as needed.
4. After the rows are joined, edgestitch around the outer edge for added durability.

lap coverlet

The hexagons in this project feature a pieced design, faced and stitched together to create the coverlet. Piecing is a fun way to add interest to the hexagon shape.

Finished size: 60" x 80" ● **Hexagon size:** 11" diameter ● **Skill level:** Advanced
Made by Jen Eskridge.

Materials

Yardage is based on 42"-wide fabric. Fat quarters measure 18" x 21".

- 2¼ yards of white solid for hexagons
- 8 fat quarters of assorted prints for hexagons
- 4 yards *total* of assorted flannel pieces for facing

Fabrics: Tilly by Daisy Janie Organic Fabrics

Cutting

From *each* of the assorted fat quarters, cut:
6 strips, 3" x 21" (48 total)

From the white solid, cut:
24 strips, 3" x 42"

⬡ piecing hexagons

The quilt on page 59 was made using the described method. Feel free to apply the faced-hexagon coverlet method to any pieced-hexagon pattern you may already own and love.

Making the Coverlet

1. Join matching assorted strips end to end to make three 3" x 42" strips from each fabric (24 total). Press the seam allowances open.

⬡ selvages

Don't cut off the selvage edge of the fat-quarter strips. Simply use that end to join the strips; it will be discarded later.

2. Join an assorted strip to the long edge of a white strip to make a strip set. Press the seam allowances toward the white strip. Repeat to make a total of 24 strip sets.

3. Fold the strip in half and align the raw edges. Align the 60° line on your ruler with the edge of the strip set. Cut along the edge of the ruler and discard the scrap triangles. Cut a total of 12 pieced 60° triangles. (You can also use a 60° triangle ruler to cut the 12 triangles.)

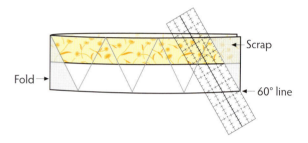

4. Arrange six matching triangles to make a hexagon. Sew three triangles together to make a half hexagon. Press the seam allowances to one side. Then join two half hexagons and press the seam allowances to one side. Use care when stitching so you don't stretch the fabrics, as every seam line is on the bias. Make 24

hexagons with white centers and 24 hexagons with white edges.

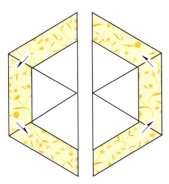

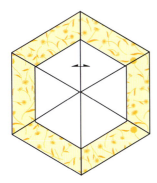

Make 24.

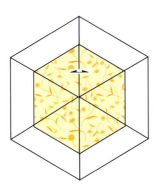

Make 24.

5. Measure the completed hexagons from corner to corner; they should measure 11½". Mark that size hexagon on the wrong side of the flannel fabric. Cut out the hexagons on the marked line.

6. Referring to "Reversible Hexagons" (page 11) and using a ¼"-wide seam allowance, make 48 reversible hexagons. The finished hexagons should now measure 11" from corner to corner. Don't worry if your hexagons are slightly larger or smaller; just make sure they are all the same size.

● optional layer

Consider adding a layer of lightweight batting or using two layers of flannel to make the coverlet warmer. Additional fabric or batting is not included in the materials list.

7. Lay out the hexagons in eight rows of six hexagons each. Butt the hexagons next to each other and use a narrow zigzag stitch to join the hexagons in each row as described in "Joining Hexagons" (page 14).

8. Use a narrow zigzag stitch to join the rows, pivoting the piece 60° at each corner, as needed.

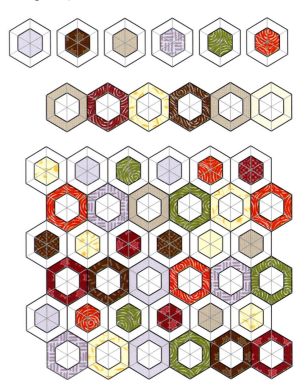

Quilt assembly

9. After the rows are joined, edgestitch around the outer edge for added durability.

Back of lap coverlet

Home-Decor Projects

This section focuses on how the facing technique can be used to make or enhance items to accent your home. These projects are faster than some of the larger, quilted projects and require less fabric. Home-decor projects are unique in that you can use a variety of fabric types to achieve a certain look for your home. The facing technique makes working with non-quilt fabric fast and easy.

Hexagons can be added to any factory-made home-decor item. Consider adding hexagons to shower curtains, pillowcases, dish and guest towels, duvets, and tailored valances. Trace the hexagon onto a piece of paper to determine which size will best fit the purchased item. You can use the paper hexagon to determine placement as well as the quantity of shapes needed.

When finishing any of the home-decor projects, consider adding performance fabrics, such as Insul-Brite or Insul-Fleece to make table runners heat resistant. Stiff sew-in interfacing is used in the banner to help the fabric maintain a crisp shape.

blocks to pillows

You can turn any of the block patterns (page 21) into a throw pillow. There are two pillow styles: plain and quilted. The sizes provided are for a finished 15" square pillow, made from a finished 15" x 15" block.

Turn a block into a throw pillow.

Plain Pillow

Feature your quilt blocks on your favorite chair or couch with this quick envelope-pillow method. The pillow shown uses block 10 (page 29).

Finished size: 15" x 15"

Hexagon sizes: 12" diameter and 4½" diameter

Skill level: Beginner

Made by Jen Eskridge.

Materials

- 1 block, 15½" x 15½"
- ⅜ yard of fabric for backing
- 15" x 15" pillow form (If you want a fuller pillow, use a 16" x 16" pillow form.)

Fabrics: Pinfeathers by Carina Gardner for Northcott Fabrics

Cutting

From the backing fabric, cut:
2 pieces, 11" x 15½"

Instructions

1. To make the pillow back, fold over ½" on one 15½" edge of both backing rectangles, and then fold over ½" again. Press and machine stitch along the folded edge.

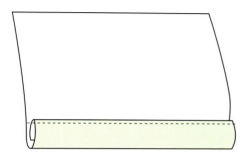

2. Overlap the hemmed edges approximately 4" to create a 15½" square. Baste the pieces along each side as shown, about ⅛" from the outer edges.

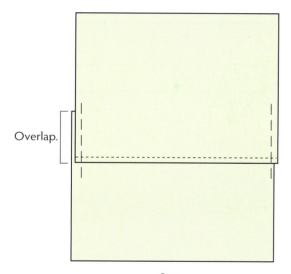

Overlap.

Baste.

3. Lay the pillow back right sides together with the block. Pin and then stitch around the edges using a ¼"-wide seam allowance.

4. Clip the corners and turn the pillow right side out; press. Insert the pillow form through the opening.

In a casual home, make the quilt block stand out with dynamic quilting. The pillow shown uses block 11 (page 30).

Finished size: 15" x 15"

Hexagon size: 9" diameter

Skill level: Beginner

Made and machine quilted by Jen Eskridge.

Materials

- 1 block, 15½" x 15½"
- ½ yard of fabric for back of quilted block and back of pillow
- ⅛ yard of fabric for binding
- 16" x 16" square of batting
- 15" x 15" pillow form (If you want a fuller pillow, use a 16" x 16" pillow form.)

Fabrics: Pinfeathers by Carina Gardner for Northcott Fabrics

Cutting

From the backing fabric, cut:
1 square, 16" x 16"
2 rectangles, 11" x 15½"

From the binding fabric, cut:
2 strips, 2" x 42"

Instructions

1. Layer the quilt block with the batting and the 16" square of backing fabric. Pin-baste the layers together, placing a pin every 4". Quilt as desired.

Quilting idea

2. Trim the backing and batting even with the edges of the quilt block. (The block may be slightly smaller after quilting.) Machine baste around the block about ⅛" from the outer edges.

3. To make the pillow back, fold over ½" on one 15½" edge of both backing rectangles, and then fold over ½" again. Press and machine stitch along the folded edge.

4. Overlap the hemmed edges to make a square that is the same size as the pillow front. Baste the pieces along each side about ⅛" from the outer edges.

5. Layer the pillow back with the pillow front, *wrong* sides together. (The pillow front will be right side out.) Pin and then machine baste around the edges of the block.

6. Join the binding strips end to end to make a long strip. Use the long strip to make and attach binding to the edges of the pillow. Insert the pillow form through the opening.

table runners

The rectangular-shaped runners in this section may also be turned into full quilts by simply repeating the runner as if it were a quilt row.

Table runners are "visual" rather than "actual" rectangles, which means large or small hexagons can be joined to create the same visual effect as a rectangular table runner.

Rows to Runners

One row of 15" blocks makes a great table runner. Consider using any four blocks to create your own design. Here, block 7 (page 28) is repeated four times, each with a different bold, solid color. The white half hexagons unify the design. Remember, table runners don't necessarily need quilting to be a finished table accent.

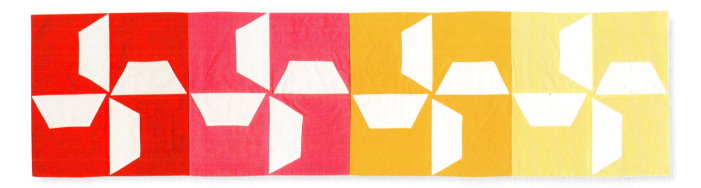

Finished size: 15" x 60"
Hexagon size: 7½" diameter
Skill level: Intermediate
Made by Jen Eskridge.

Materials

- 4 squares, 8" x 8", *each* of 4 assorted solid fabrics for background
- ⅝ yard of white solid for hexagons
- ⅝ yard of fabric for facing
- 17" x 62" piece of fabric for backing

Making the Table Runner

1. Refer to the detailed instructions and illustrations on page 28 to make four of block 7.
2. Join the four blocks to complete the table runner top. Press the seam allowances open.
3. Center the table runner on top of the backing, right sides together, and pin in place. Using a ¼"-wide seam allowance, stitch all the way around the outer edge, leaving a 6" opening for turning. Note that there is no batting in this table runner.
4. Trim the excess backing even with the table runner. Turn the table runner right sides out through the opening. Use a blind stitch to sew the opening closed.

Dress up any formal dining table with the elegance of silk. Using the facing technique allows a range of fabric options when home decor and quilting collide.

Materials

- ⅞ yard of 54"-wide white silk shantung for background and binding
- 36 pieces, at least 4" x 4", of assorted silk fabrics for hexagons*
- ½ yard of fabric for facing
- 18" x 50" piece of fabric for backing
- 18" x 50" piece of batting

Fabrics: Magnolia Silks

*The fabrics in this sample are from an interior designer's fabric swatch book. To make a table runner for a more casual dining room, use assorted 5" squares of 100% cotton fabrics.

Finished size: 16" x 48"
Hexagon size: 3½" diameter
Skill level: Beginner
Made by Jen Eskridge and machine quilted by Colleen Eskridge.

Cutting

From the white silk shantung, cut:
1 piece, 18" x 50"
3 binding strips, 2½" x 54"

Making the Table Runner

Refer to "Preparing the Facing Hexagons" (page 10) and "Appliquéd Hexagons" (page 12) for detailed instructions as needed.

1. Prepare 36 assorted 3½"-diameter hexagons for appliqué.
2. Arrange the hexagons on the white-silk background in 12 rows of three hexagons each, leaving a consistent ¾" to 1" space between each hexagon. This will create a sashing effect. Pin the hexagons in place, moving them around until you are pleased with the arrangement. The colors in the sample on the facing page are graded using the color wheel as a guide.

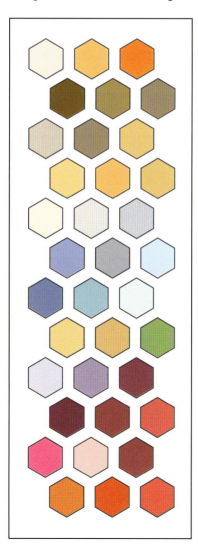

3. Use an edgestitch to appliqué the hexagons in place. Carefully press the appliquéd piece.

⬡ use a stabilizer

When working with unique fabrics that may fray, consider stabilizing the fabrics with a lightweight fusible interfacing. This will also reduce any shifting in fabric grain as you stitch, trim, quilt, and bind the project.

Finishing the Quilt

For more information on any finishing techniques, please visit ShopMartingale.com/HowtoQuilt to download free illustrated how-to instructions.

1. Layer the table runner, batting, and backing; baste the layers together. Quilt as desired.
2. Bind the table runner using the 2½"-wide binding strips, and then add a label.

Peekaboo Table Runner

Create a unique, scattered look in this table-runner design with open windows. Use the windows to peek through at the table, frame candles and centerpieces, or showcase lace and crocheted table cloths. This table runner is a fun gift idea and a great project for digging into your scrap stash.

Finished size: 15" x 40" • **Hexagon size:** 4½" diameter • **Skill level:** Intermediate
Made by Jen Eskridge.

Materials

- 52 squares, 5" x 5" of assorted prints for hexagons

Fabrics: Terrain by Kate Spain for Moda Fabrics

⬡ colors

Before starting to sew, sort the hexagons into color families, so your reversible runner will have one color family on one side and a coordinating color family on the reverse side.

Instructions

Refer to "Preparing the Facing Hexagons" (page 10) and "Reversible Hexagons" (page 11) for detailed instructions as needed.

1. Prepare 26 assorted 4½"-diameter reversible hexagons.
2. On a flat surface, arrange six hexagons in a ring as shown. Using a narrow zigzag stitch and coordinating thread, join the hexagons as described in "Joining Hexagons" (page 14). Make three rings.

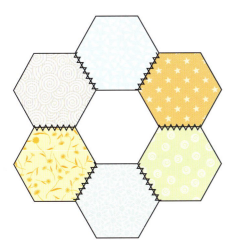

⬡ thread color

If the hexagons represent a wide range of colors, choose gray thread to blend with both sides of the design.

3. In the same manner, join the three rings. Then add the remaining hexagons as shown to complete the table runner.

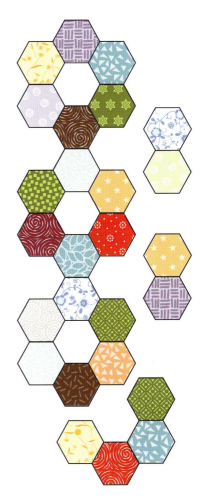

Turn a favorite decorator-weight fabric into a versatile—and reversible—table runner using only seven hexagons.

Finished size: 18" x 62" • **Hexagon sizes:** 18" diameter and 9" diameter • **Skill level:** Beginner
Made by Jen Eskridge.

Materials

- 1½ yards of 54"-wide decorator-weight fabric for large hexagons
- 3 squares, 10" x 10", of assorted solid cotton fabrics for small hexagons
- ¼ yard *total* of fabric for facing
- 1 yard of ½"-wide grosgrain ribbon

Fabrics: Korean decorator fabric and Kona Solids by Robert Kaufman Fabrics

Instructions

Refer to "Preparing the Facing Hexagons" (page 10), "Reversible Hexagons" (page 11), and "Appliquéd Hexagons" (page 12) for detailed instructions as needed. Although the project is reversible, each side will be finished differently.

1. Using the decorator-weight fabric, prepare four 18"-diameter reversible hexagons using the same fabric on both sides. Using the cotton fabrics, prepare three assorted 9"-diameter hexagons for appliqué.

2. Use a zigzag stitch to join the large hexagons side by side as described in "Joining Hexagons" (page 14). Rotate the hexagons, as needed, to make sure the open edges are securely closed with the zigzag stitching. The stitching will be covered, so you don't need to use matching thread.

3. Cut the ribbon into three 12"-long pieces. On one side, center the ribbon over the zigzag stitching, completely covering the joined seam. Wrap the ends of the ribbon around the edges of the hexagon about 1½" as shown. Use thread that matches the ribbon and straight

stitch along both edges of the ribbon. Repeat the process on each joined seam.

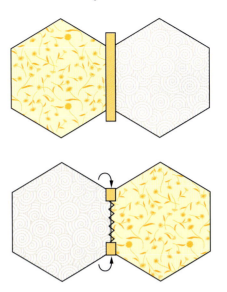

Fold ribbon around edges.

4. On the other side of the table runner, position a small hexagon on top of each joined seam. The small hexagons are positioned with the points aligned on the seam line. Pin in place. Edgestitch the small hexagons to the table runner.

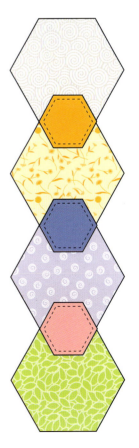

hot pads

Hot pads are a sweet, quick home gift item. They're great for holidays, housewarming gifts, and swap projects.

Finished size: 9" diameter
Skill level: Beginner
Made by Jen Eskridge.

● fabrics

1 fat quarter will make two matching 9"-diameter hexagon hot pads.

Materials

Yields 1 hot pad

- 2 squares, 11" x 11", of fabric for hexagons*
- 1 rectangle, 2" x 5", of fabric for loop*
- 11" x 11" square of Insul-Brite

Fabrics: Tokyo Rocco by Carol Van Zandt for Andover Fabrics

You can use one focus fabric throughout or a different focus fabric for each piece.

Instructions

Refer to "Preparing the Facing Hexagons" (page 10) for detailed instructions as needed. Instructions are for one hot pad.

1. To make the loop, fold over both long edges of the focus fabric rectangle ¼" to the wrong side and press.

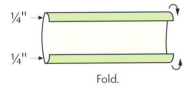

Fold.

2. Fold the rectangle in half lengthwise, with the folded edges aligned, and press. Edgestitch along both folds.

3. Trace a 9"-diameter hexagon onto the wrong side of one focus fabric square. Insert a pin in the corner of the marked hexagon, placing the pin perpendicular to the corner and making sure you can see it from the right side of the square. Fold the loop in half and baste the cut ends to the pinned corner of the hexagon, on the right side of the square. The loop should point

toward the center of the hexagon, opposite of how it will look when the project is finished.

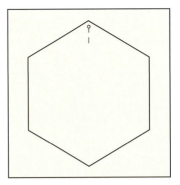

4. Place the unmarked square of focus fabric on top of the Insul-Brite square. With right sides together, layer the marked square on top of the focus fabric square. Pin the layers together. Stitch around the hexagon as described in "Reversible Hexagons" (page 11).

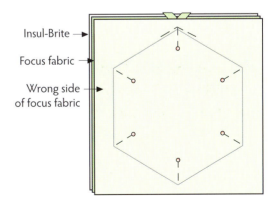

Insul-Brite →

Focus fabric →

Wrong side of focus fabric →

5. Clip the corners. Trim the seam allowances to ¼" wide. Turn the hexagon right side out and press. Edgestitch around the outer edge to close the opening.

joy banner

Personalize any party or holiday with this fun, quick banner, and get more for your effort, as the project is reversible.

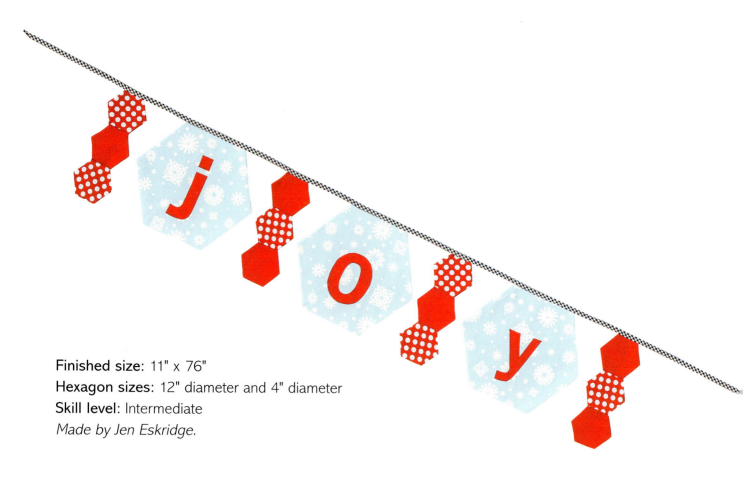

Finished size: 11" x 76"

Hexagon sizes: 12" diameter and 4" diameter

Skill level: Intermediate

Made by Jen Eskridge.

banners and buntings

This banner can be customized to accommodate any word or name, and it's strung together using premade double-fold bias tape. If you choose a longer or shorter word, it will require yardage adjustments (not provided).

The banner presented here is made from 100% cotton fabrics, interfaced with heavy sew-in interfacing. It is made using the reversible facing technique, since the banner may hang in a window or doorway.

Materials

- ⅜ yard of blue print for large hexagons
- ⅜ yard of red polka-dot fabric for small hexagons
- ⅜ yard of red solid for small hexagons
- ⅜ yard of gray print for facing
- 1½ yard of heavy-weight sew-in interfacing
- ⅓ yard of fusible web
- 1 package of ½"-wide double-fold bias tape

make your own

Premade bias tape can be found in the notions area of a fabric store and is generally used for dressmaking. You can use a 1"-wide bias-tape maker to make your own double-fold bias tape, following the manufacturer's directions. Then press the 1"-wide strip in half lengthwise to make ½"-wide bias tape.

Instructions

1. Trace three 12"-diameter hexagons onto the *wrong* side of the blue print and the gray print. Trace six 12" diameter hexagons onto the interfacing. Cut out the hexagons, leaving a ½" margin all around the marked line.

2. Using a long running stitch, hand baste the interfacing to the wrong side of each blue hexagon and each gray hexagon, making sure the marked line on the interfacing is visible.

3. Layer a blue hexagon with a gray hexagon, right sides together, and sew on the marked line as described in "Reversible Hexagons" (page 11). Clip the corners and trim the seam allowances to ¼" wide. Turn the hexagons right side out.

4. Referring to "Preparing the Facing Hexagons" (page 10) and "Reversible Hexagons," make 12 red 4"-diameter hexagons. Each reversible hexagon should have red solid on one side and red polka-dot fabric on the other side.

5. Open the word-processing program on your computer. Choose a font with thick letters, such as a size 600 Century Gothic or Gautami font. Type the word *joy* and apply bold formatting to the word. Print the word; each letter should fill a sheet of paper. You may need to adjust the size of the margins to avoid cropping the letters when printing.

6. Use a pencil to trace the letters *in reverse* onto the paper side of the fusible web. Following the manufacturer's instructions, press the fusible web with the traced letters to the wrong side of the remaining red solid.

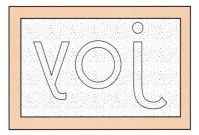

7. Use scissors to cut out the letters, cutting directly on the traced lines. Remove the paper backing. Making sure the opening of the hexagon is at the top, position and fuse a letter in the center of each blue hexagon.

8. Using a narrow zigzag stitch and red thread, join three small hexagons as described in "Joining Hexagons" (page 14). Alternate the red solid and red polka-dot fabric as shown in the photo on page 76 and rotate the hexagons, as needed, to make sure the open edges are securely closed with the zigzag stitching. Make four.

9. Cut a 76"-long piece of bias tape and mark the center with a pin. Mark the center on the "O" hexagon with a pin. Matching the center marks, tuck the hexagon into the bias tape, so that the bias tape covers both sides of the hexagon. Securely pin in place. Keep in mind that you'll need to catch the bottom layer of the bias tape as you sew, so make sure you pin through all of the fabric layers.

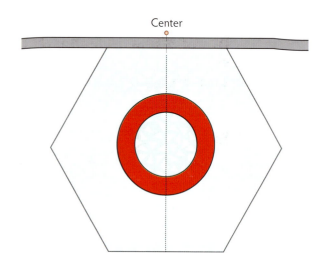

10. Arrange a column of red hexagons, a large appliquéd hexagon, and then another column of red hexagons on each side of the center hexagon, making sure they are equidistant from each other. Securely pin in place through all of the fabric layers.

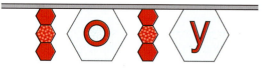

11. Carefully stitch along the entire length of the bias tape, making sure to sew through both layers of bias tape.

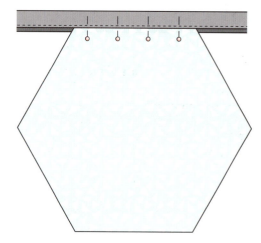

12. Tie a simple knot at each end of the bias tape to create a finished look.

resources and acknowledgments

Many of the supplies listed below can be found at your local quilt or craft shop. If you can't find them locally, try these websites.

General Supplies

60° triangle ruler by Creative Grids
CreativeGridsUSA.com

Adobe Photoshop
Adobe.com

Hexagon dies by AccuQuilt
AccuQuilt.com

Bias-tape maker by Clover
Clover-USA.com

Hexagon ruler by Darlene Zimmerman for EZ Quilting
Simplicity.com

Inklingo
Inklingo.com

Fabrics

Andover Fabrics
AndoverFabrics.com

Art Gallery Fabrics
ArtGalleryFabrics.com

Daisy Janie
DaisyJanie.com

FreeSpirit
FreeSpiritFabric.com

Kona Cotton Solids by Robert Kaufmann Fabrics
RobertKaufman.com

Moda Fabrics
ModaFabrics.com

Northcott Fabrics
Northcott.net

Rowan Fabric
WestminsterFabrics.com

Studio E Fabrics
StudioEFabrics.com

Acknowledgments

Special thanks to the following long-arm quilters: Evelyn Gernaat, Celebrity Quilting/CelebrityQuilting.com; Karen Morello/Karens-Quilting-Service.blogspot.com; Colleen Eskridge/Yackity-Yak.blogspot.com

about the author

Designer Jen Eskridge is a native Texan who has lived and traveled all over the world. Her favorite residence to date is Daegu, South Korea. The longest she has lived anywhere—since college in Baton Rouge—has only been three years.

It was in South Korea, while shopping at fabric manufacturers' mill markets, that Jen decided to apply her apparel design degree to her very own quilting and sewing pattern company, ReannaLily Designs. Once she returned to the United States in 2008, Jen launched the company with commissioned sewing jobs and her trademarked Seamingly Accurate Seam Guide. ReannaLily Designs has evolved into a pattern and design company in addition to its sewing beginnings. It is largely focused on quick, affordable designs for sewing enthusiasts of all skill levels.

Jen maintains a daily blog to showcase sewing adventures, successes, and mishaps. Visit her at ReannaLilyDesigns.com/blog. Her design work has been featured in numerous quilting magazines as well as television and radio shows. This is her second book and she was a contributing artist in a few other titles.

What's your creative passion?
Find it at ShopMartingale.com

books • eBooks • ePatterns • daily blog • free projects
videos • tutorials • inspiration • giveaways

Martingale®
Create with Confidence